Betty Shine was born in Kennington in 1929. Her grandmother was a spiritualist. Before she became a practising healer she was a professional singer, and she has at times taught vitamin and mineral therapy, hand analysis and yoga. She lives and practises near the south coast. She is also the author of *Mind Magic*, *Mind Waves* and *Betty Shine's Mind Workbook*, which are also published by Corgi.

Also by Betty Shine

MIND MAGIC
MIND WAVES
BETTY SHINE'S MIND WORKBOOK

and published by Corgi Books

Betty Shine

MIND TO MIND

The Secrets of Your Mind Energy Revealed

Edited by Anthea Courtenay

Foreword by Michael Bentine

CORGI BOOKS

MIND TO MIND
A CORGI BOOK : 0 552 13378 7

Originally published in Great Britain by Bantam Press

PRINTING HISTORY
Bantam Press edition published 1989
Corgi edition published 1990
Corgi edition reprinted 1991 (twice)
Corgi edition reprinted 1992
Corgi edition reprinted 1993
Corgi edition reprinted 1994
Corgi edition reprinted 1995
Corgi edition reprinted 1996
Corgi edition reprinted 1997

Grateful acknowledgement is made for permission to reprint
from *Patterns in Nature* by Peter S. Stevens.
Copyright © 1974 by Peter S. Stevens
By permission of Little, Brown and Company.

Condition of Sale

This book is set in 10/11pt Linotron 202 Sabon by
Rowland Phototypesetting Ltd, Bury St Edmunds, Suffolk.

Corgi Books are published by Transworld Publishers Ltd,
61–63 Uxbridge Road, London W5 5SA,
in Australia by Transworld Publishers (Australia) Pty Ltd,
15–25 Helles Avenue, Moorebank, NSW 2170,
and in New Zealand by Transworld Publishers (NZ) Ltd,
3 William Pickering Drive, Albany, Auckland.

Printed and bound in Great Britain by
Cox & Wyman Ltd, Reading, Berkshire.

*This book is dedicated to Janet,
my daughter and my friend*

Contents

FOREWORD

My close friend Betty Shine has an appropriate surname. Good humour, bubbling energy and down-to-earth honesty seem to radiate from her warm and attractive personality, making her any child's idea of the perfect aunty.

Over the years, Betty has been kind enough to give me healing on many occasions. Usually, I arrive at her home with my energy reserves seriously depleted and in a low state of health. When I leave her, I invariably feel marvellously renewed, refreshed and once again ready to continue whatever task life has set for me. For those healing sessions and for her cheerful loyal friendship I shall always be in her debt.

No matter how remarkable you may consider the evidence in this book to be, it cannot convey all the extraordinary abilities and gifts which Betty has in abundance. To appreciate these rare qualities you must meet her yourself. If you are lucky enough to do so, you will know exactly what I mean.

Betty Shine has many things to say. These are the results of years of concentrated effort and hard work. Being Betty, my friend writes in the same way that she thinks and speaks: straight out, with no mumbo-jumbo.

This is a rare book, written by a rare person. I know that you will enjoy reading it, many times.

My wife and I will never forget the look of blessed relief on our daughter Marylla's face when, despite long journeys throughout the storms of that grim winter, Betty came many miles to give her healing. Although she was unable to halt the process of the cancer, which eventually caused Marylla's premature death, Betty Shine brought our child something very precious: the gift of comfort and mental peace. For that alone I can never thank her enough.

Betty, my dear friend, may this book help many others, as you have so often helped us.

Bless you and those who work with you.

MICHAEL BENTINE

PROLOGUE

A Journey of Enlightenment

In the beginning was the Word
The spoken Word
and much later the written Word
Communication depends on words
There would be no progress
without them
and the words in this book
are the golden threads
that continue to weave a
story from the beginning of
man to the present day.

BETTY SHINE

'Come in, Betty. Your mother, Alice, has been waiting for you.'

I had just entered a darkened room lit by the glow of a small red lamp, and a tall slim man was shaking my hand. I had never visited a medium before, and I had only come because I was desperate. Now I nearly ran away. Charles Horrey looked kindly enough – but how on earth did he know my first name, let alone the name of my mother who had been dead for five years?

As soon as I was seated, he said: 'Your mother has been wanting to communicate with you for a long time. She would like to ask your forgiveness.'

I was startled; I already knew that my mother had been trying to communicate with me, but I couldn't think of anything I had to forgive her for.

Mr Horrey went on: 'She says she could have given you

more time.' That did make some sense. 'Now she is giving you something you always wanted, but in a different way.'

'What is it?' I asked.

'I don't know. . .' For a few moments Mr Horrey sat in silence, his head tilted as though listening. Then he said: 'You are going to be a great healer.'

Me – a healer? This was ridiculous! It wasn't what I'd come to hear at all. How could I heal others when I was ill myself?

My thoughts raced as he leaned forward. 'You have been ill for seven years.'

That was true. I had decided to see a medium because I had been troubled for the last few years by inexplicable attacks of dizziness and palpitations; lately they had been getting worse, and I was afraid I was going to die.

He went on: 'You have been a very obstinate woman. A doctor has been trying to work through you all this time, and you haven't been listening. This is what has made you ill; because you haven't been using the healing energy it has built up in your system. Once you start healing you will be better.'

Then he delivered another bombshell. 'You are also a medium and you have been developing your mediumship through the focus that was chosen for you: hand-reading.' It was true that for many years I had been doing medical hand analysis for friends – but mediumship? 'This will now stop. In future you will have the knowledge without using the hand as a focus.'

My expression must have shown how I felt about becoming a medium. Mr Horrey looked at me quite sternly, so I sat quietly listening to the rest of his message.

'In the next three months you will not only have the ability to see spirit people; you will also hear them.' He didn't know, of course, that I had already seen spirit people more than once. 'You will have clairvoyant sight and will be able to diagnose illnesses.'

I'd never thought of myself as anything but an ordinary unimportant person. I looked at him and said: 'I couldn't sit in a room with a little red light all day; it would drive me crackers!'

'My dear girl,' he said, 'that happens to be my choice. You may choose your own way of working. You will not work from the platform; all of your work will be confidential.'

Then he took my hand and held it while he said: 'Remember everything you have been told. There are many psychics in the world, but few are chosen.'

I thought: Whoever does the choosing must have made a mistake; I'm sure they've got the wrong one! My picture of psychics simply didn't tally with my picture of myself.

Mr Horrey looked at me a little sadly. 'You know, it doesn't give me any pleasure telling you this. It's an extremely difficult path to follow, and you will have to spend the rest of your life helping others. It's not a job I would have chosen. Like you, I had no choice but, unlike yourself, I can only sit here passing on messages. I could never heal; I don't have that kind of power.'

'But how the hell can I heal people?' I burst out.

'You already *are* healing people!' he told me. 'You've been holding people's hands when you read them, haven't you? Well, you've been healing them! Go away and try it.'

The whole sitting lasted about an hour. Mr Horrey told me more about my past, my future, my healing career — there was so much that I really couldn't take it all in. It was all totally unexpected and rather frightening.

As he drew to a close, he told me: 'You are the most powerful psychic I have ever met in the thirty years I have been doing this work, and you have a great future as a healer. You will achieve incredible results, and you will travel all over the world.'

I stumbled out into the daylight and reeled back to work, wondering what on earth I was going to tell my husband and daughter. Back in my office, unable to concentrate, I went over and over the conversation in my head, trying to make sense of it. I was beginning to see myself in a new light. I had never thought of myself as psychic. Yet I realized that many of the things which had happened to me, which I had taken for granted, other people might consider very strange – psychic, in fact.

I had no idea that from this point on my life would never be the same again. Although Mr Horrey had given me some extraordinarily accurate information about myself, I knew nothing about healing and had no intention of becoming a healer. I certainly had no idea that, at the age of forty-six, I was about to embark on a whole new career.

Not until much later was I able to look back calmly and see that from the start my whole life had been directed and guided towards this end: that I had in fact been on a journey, which I now think of as a journey of enlightenment.

For as long as I could remember, I had been visiting another dimension. When I was two I smashed my forehead in a fall, affecting the optic nerve and necessitating an operation. Perhaps the blow to the head triggered my psychic abilities; whatever the cause, one minute I was lying in a hospital cot, the next I found myself in a totally different place.

I was in a garden full of colour: there were flowers like no flowers on earth, with huge, brilliantly coloured trumpets which I could have crawled down, and exotic, brightly plumed birds with long tails. The colours shimmered, constantly changing in tone: a flower would be deep orange one moment and pale apricot when I looked again.

It was a remarkable and very beautiful experience that has been repeated continuously throughout my life, changing in certain details as my life has changed. From that time onwards, whenever I wanted to, I could just close my eyes and travel to this magical place.

As soon as I entered it I would find myself walking down a narrow path which wound between a tall hedge of plants, seemingly placed there to prevent me from seeing what was beyond. At one point, to my right I would pass a rectangular pool round which sat groups of people in long robes, silently communicating with each other. Some people were being dipped in the water, as if they were being baptized.

I never walked to the pool, but kept to the path as though I had an appointment. I would pass under an arch of leaves and then turn right to climb up a grassy slope, which felt soft and springy underfoot. At the top I would enter a small hexagonal building with a domed roof; inside, it was light and very peaceful.

From the first, I had an inner knowledge of what to do. I would go to a chair, sit down and wait. After a while, someone would enter and sit behind me. Though I never looked round, I somehow knew that this person had a thin face, kindly eyes and long light-brown hair. He had no name and he never spoke; we simply sat in silence. What seemed like moments later, I would stand up and leave. Instantly I would find myself back in the 'real' world.

My early childhood was very happy. I was born in Kennington ten years before the start of the Second World War, the middle child of three. My mother was very loving, deeply religious, and blessed with a sense of humour. My father worked in the hotel business, which meant that we saw very little of him in the evenings and even at weekends; but he was a very caring man and a lovely father. He came from a family of artists, singers and musicians; he was a gifted amateur artist himself. We lived in a working-class community of terraced houses, a secure environment in which all the families knew and cared about each other.

The highlight of the week was Sunday, when my father took the three of us to see his mother, who lived in an imposing Victorian house in Kennington Lane. A small woman with a powerful personality and great courage, she had given birth to thirteen children, several of whom had died young. A life-long spiritualist, she was very psychic and used to hold long conversations with her dead sons which she would relate to us when we arrived on our weekly visits. Since we grew up with this we accepted it as normal; my father seemed to accept it, too, although not a spiritualist himself.

I found my grandmother fascinating. She often made accurate predictions about future events; even my mother had to admit that she was often right, although spiritualism was quite at odds with her High Church beliefs. Sometimes I, too, knew when things were going to happen. I remember telling my mother, correctly, that a neighbour was going to die. She told me quite sharply not to say such things; I think she felt that by voicing them I was actually bringing them about. Anything smacking of the psychic terrified her.

I loved going to church, not because I was particularly religious but because I welcomed any opportunity to sing. When I was about eight my mother was horrified one Sunday to find me singing in the street with the Salvation Army! I was thoroughly enjoying myself, and was mortified when she dragged me away in disgrace. Not only was I singing in the street, but with the Salvation Army of all things!

At school and at home I was always being told off for day-dreaming; it was so easy to slip into my other world for a few minutes that I did it without thinking. Sometimes my mother would say: 'You've been somewhere else, haven't you?' But when I told her about my journeys she dismissed them as day-dreams.

I know now that my garden was and is absolutely real, existing in another dimension. I also know that during my visits there I was being taught telepathically by my silent companion, for when I returned I would be aware of things that no one else had taught me. For example, I understood as a very small child the spiritual law that whatever you give out you get back. This made me very anxious when I heard my mother running down a friend behind her back; I knew that it would hurt *her*, and told her so!

I always felt extremely close to nature: I could hear the trees talking to each other, and when I lay on the ground in our local park I could hear the grass growing. When I told my mother this, she used to laugh at my imagination. Later, in the country, I felt the streams were talking to me.

From a very early age I could also hear a man's voice speaking softly in my ear from time to time; I knew that he was a different person from my silent teacher. He was very protective: he would say 'Stop!' as I was about to run across a road without looking, or before I did something forbidden at school; at other times he reassured me when my courage was failing, or gave me advice about my school work.

I never connected these experiences with my grandmother's psychic powers or my mother's religious beliefs. My grandmother's discussions about her dead sons were always very matter-of-fact, and she never mentioned spirits. My mother told me that we all have a guardian angel who is always with us – an idea I found quite terrifying. I used to look round for it, thinking it was disapprovingly watching everything I did.

My protective voice was simply a normal part of life, and I assumed that everyone heard voices. Then, when I was about eight, I mentioned to my best friend something 'this man' had said. 'What man?' she asked.

'This man who speaks to me. Haven't you got a man speaking to you?'

'No,' said my friend, giving me an odd look. 'That sounds really weird!'

I was genuinely surprised to learn that she didn't have a person, but from then on I kept quiet about mine.

My first ten years were perhaps the happiest of my life. Then came the war. The next thing I knew, we were being evacuated, sent to the country for our safety away from the London bombs.

My brother and sister went together, but for some

reason I was evacuated on my own. For me and many others, it was the beginning of a nightmare. Dazed by the whole situation, not understanding what 'war' meant, I found myself with hundreds of other children being piled on to a train. From time to time I looked out of the window: until then my horizons had consisted of rows and rows of houses and the local park. The country was obviously a huge park without railings.

We arrived at a small Berkshire village which seemed like the end of the world. We were met by a billeting officer, who handed each of us a bar of Cadbury's chocolate – I'd never had such a large bar of chocolate to myself! He then trailed us round from one home to another, finally taking me to what seemed a very large house, where I was introduced to the lady and gentleman who were to look after me. The house was very gloomy, and Mr and Mrs E seemed very old; they must actually have been in their sixties.

The first thing Mrs E did was to take my bar of chocolate. I never saw it again. I was shocked; stealing was a terrible thing to do, and this lady had stolen my bar of chocolate. Her husband, Tom, looked sympathetic, but under his wife's steely gaze was clearly afraid to say very much. I was afraid, too, and with good reason.

Life with these people was wretched: physically and emotionally, I was starved. I was only given hot food at weekends when Mr E was at home; it was cooked on a little meths-stove, and always tasted of methylated spirits. I walked two miles to school every day with rhubarb sandwiches for my midday meal; my tea consisted of two pieces of bread and margarine, and on Wednesdays a piece of lardy cake.

If I dared ask for more, the Lady, as I thought of her, would tell me that she was given half a crown a week for my keep, and that was all I was going to get! I was too frightened to tell anyone, least of all my mother, in case I was sent to bed with no food at all. I remember the hunger to this day.

At school, which was held in a church hall, I learned that some of my fellow-evacuees were happy and comfortable. Others were very miserable and homesick. Many, including myself, were treated as servants by the people to whom they had been entrusted. I had to do housework when I came home from school, and spent Saturday mornings polishing every single piece of cutlery and silver! The Lady only spoke to me to give me orders.

One Sunday I tried to run away; I had walked two miles before Tom E caught up with me and took me back. He told me I would get no Sunday lunch, but for some reason this threat wasn't carried out. Perhaps, after all, the Lady had a conscience, or perhaps Tom intervened on my behalf.

One night, about four months after my arrival, a bomb dropped immediately opposite the house, shattering all the windows. There was no electric light in my room, as Mrs E was too mean to put blackout in the upstairs windows. When she came in with a candle I saw a piece of glass quivering like a spear in the headboard, an inch above my head. I thought: I could have been killed!

I believe the shock must have opened up my psychic awareness. One evening about a week after the blast, I was lying in bed in the dark when suddenly somebody walked in through the closed door. I stared, transfixed; I could make out the shape of a person – whether man or woman, I couldn't tell. It was followed by others: streams of shadowy-looking people began walking across the room and out through the opposite wall.

My first thought was that when they walked through the outer wall they would drop to the ground outside and do themselves an injury. Someone ought to warn them! Then I became scared. Not daring to disturb the Lady, I pulled the sheet over my head, hoping whoever they were would go away, but whenever I popped up for air they were still there. I must have fallen asleep at some point, but I felt as though I was awake all night.

This visitation was repeated nearly every night; eventually I became quite used to my 'misty people' and even quite friendly towards them. Although they ignored me, having people of my very own was a kind of comfort. Especially since, while they were about, I had lost another source of comfort; I could no longer hear the voice of my invisible friend, who had so often spoken reassuringly in my ear.

The probable explanation for this, although I could not know it then, is that these experiences were all normal steps in my psychic development. Other mediums have been through similar stages. There will be a phase during which one's clairaudience is developed, enabling one to hear voices; this may fade for a period while clairvoyant sight develops. Then may follow a time when sight and sound disappear, and healing comes to the fore. Finally the medium has a full range of abilities on which to draw.

It seems likely that during the period of 'misty people' I was simply looking into another dimension, in which these people were going about their ordinary business. There are many dimensions in the universe, some of which can be seen by psychics with clairvoyant sight. (For a scientific comment, see page 136.) At the time, misty friends were better than none, and when I left that house they were all that I missed!

Meanwhile, I spent more and more time visiting my other-dimensional garden, and I also found another source of consolation. One evening a week Mr and Mrs E locked me out of the house until late while they went to the cinema. I would spend the hours sitting in the branches of a conifer on the corner of a country lane, looking at the stars, focusing all my attention on them until I felt that I was flying among them.

I believe that I was experiencing astral travel, that my mind was expanding and leaving my body, literally floating among the bright stars. As I floated I would hear voices speaking around me in a soft murmuring babble. They didn't seem to be speaking to me, and I couldn't really hear what they said, but it was comforting to feel I was not alone. And then, suddenly, I would be back in my tree, aware that I had been far away.

The three-years deprivation left me with an indelible emotional scar, but I also retained memories of unbelievably beautiful mystical experiences. And I learned at an early age that beauty and the beast often go hand in hand: you have to have the one to appreciate the other.

When I was thirteen my mother rented a house in Surrey, and at last the family was together again. The relief was beyond belief. But things were not the same. My father, who was still working in London, went home one day to pick up some belongings. As he turned into our street a bomb fell, reducing our house to rubble before his eyes. The blast caused what was diagnosed as 'pressure on the brain', and he became increasingly paralysed.

I, too, was in very poor health; I was literally skin and bone, and unable to eat and digest properly. The doctor told my mother I was suffering from acute malnutrition; he was appalled at my state. So was my mother, who was also, naturally, extremely angry. I was given extra rations and vouchers for cod liver oil, malt and liver, but it was eighteen months before I fully recovered.

Family life was still warm, but less companionable as my mother had to work, as well as looking after my father. I was sent to a local school, where I worked hard and managed to catch up with the rest of the girls. But I found my mind journeys much more interesting. At this time my experience changed in quality: sometimes during a lesson I would have the thrilling conviction that I had access to extraordinary knowledge. I would gaze vacantly at the teacher as I listened to other voices telling me about cosmic forces and universal energy. Sometimes I would feel that I was hovering about five hundred feet above the ground, looking down on fields and countryside.

I had always loved animals, and had longed to own a kitten, but my mother didn't share my enthusiasm and refused to have animals in the house. One day a visitor came to school to talk about opportunities for careers in the veterinary profession. At once I knew that was what I wanted to do; I had seen a number of animals ill-treated and had always wanted to help them. I raced home to ask my mother if I could become a vet. The answer was a most definite no; nothing I could say would make her change her mind! Although I eventually stopped thinking about it, much as I loved my mother I never really forgave her for that.

I left school at fourteen and went reluctantly to work in a series of offices; I could never get excited over debit and credit notes, typing and the evening post. One of my jobs was at Benson's, the advertising agency. In those days 'Benson's girls' wore smart uniforms with a little cap, which I did enjoy; it made me feel very grown-up.

I made the most of my leisure-time by going dancing in the evenings, and at one of these dances, on VE night, I met my future husband. I was sixteen; Leslie, an aircraft engineer, was two years older. For the first time I had someone with whom I could discuss serious subjects; he also shared my interest in music. I still loved singing, and used to practise arias around the house, learned from listening to the radio. It was a happy time. We were separated while Leslie did a three-year stint with the occupation forces in Germany, but before he left we got engaged.

Shortly after the war ended my father had a leucotomy to relieve the pressure on his brain. Something went terribly wrong, and when my mother next saw him he was a completely different person; my kind generous father had been left with persecution mania.

During this worrying time my grandmother took my mother to a demonstration by the famous spiritualist healer the late Harry Edwards, at Kingsway Hall in London. My mother found him so inspiring that she used to write to him at his healing-centre in Shere, and went to his lectures whenever she could. She would still never have

24

anything to do with what she called 'the occult', but she regarded healing as a religious activity rather than as the occult.

In 1947, Leslie had just come home on leave for Christmas when our happiness was suddenly shattered. The police came on Christmas morning to tell us they had found my father's possessions on Putney Embankment; he had drowned himself. On Boxing Day my mother went over to Kennington to tell my grandmother the news; as she reached the steps of the house my grandmother came out and said: 'You don't have to tell me. I went down with him.'

It was a horrible period; my father's body wasn't found for a month, and I prayed and prayed that it was all a mistake and that he was safe. Every time someone came to the door I hoped it was him.

After his death, my mother received many letters from people, often strangers, telling her how my father had helped them, often financially. We had known nothing of this. Of all my memories of my father, I remember his kindness most of all.

Soon afterwards my grandmother persuaded my mother to accompany her to a spiritualist church service with her daughter, my Aunt Lizzie. (Like my mother, Aunt Lizzie was frightened of the 'occult' and used to express her anxiety by exclaiming: 'Oh, bloomey!') Afterwards a woman approached my mother and said: 'I must tell you that there was a man standing beside you throughout the whole service.' She went on to give an exact description of my father, and then said: 'He wants you all to know that now he's very happy.'

One night about six months after his death, I woke up from a half-sleep, screaming. My father had been bending over me, apparently trying to tell me something. My mother came running into the bedroom and assured me it had only been a bad dream. I knew otherwise: the experience had been much more real than a dream.

It seems possible that my father was trying to impress

on me that I should learn as much as possible, because after recovering from the initial shock I suddenly acquired an insatiable thirst for knowledge. I joined all sorts of evening classes. It was exciting: I had only to enrol and I could learn anything I wanted. From that day to this I have never wasted a moment; I have gone on learning, and exploring the capacities of my mind.

Leslie and I married in 1949 when I was twenty, and two years later I had my first child, Geoffrey. When I was seventeen I had been in an accident on the back of Leslie's motorbike, and fourteen months after our son's birth I developed severe and continuous back-pain. I went to several hospitals, but nobody could find out what was wrong: more than one specialist told me it was 'all in my mind'.

Soon after this trouble started, I was in bed one night when I saw a tiny blue light, about the size of a penny piece, slowly travelling over the bedroom wall, across the window curtains and eventually coming to rest above my head. I pointed it out to Leslie, but he could see nothing; suddenly I had an inner certainty that my mother had asked Harry Edwards to help heal my back, and that this light was somehow connected with that. The next time I saw her she handed me a letter from his centre in Shere saying that healing would begin next day – which was the evening when the light had appeared.

That was my first encounter with absent healing. I didn't know what the blue light meant, but I knew that Harry Edwards was a very powerful healer. Although my pain continued (it was to last for seventeen more years), it was comforting to know that from somewhere in space, perhaps even from God, I was being cared for.

Four years after Geoffrey my daughter Janet was born, completing my family. I had no idea that I had given birth to another natural psychic! This birth, like the first one, was tough; on both occasions I nearly lost my life. I think that each time the stress pushed me a little further along my destined path: becoming a healer often involves going through some very difficult times.

On the positive side, marriage gave me the chance to fulfil at least one of my ambitions: early on Leslie encouraged me to go to a singing teacher, who told me that I had a dramatic coloratura voice which could be trained for opera. I thought that six months would be plenty; I had no idea that opera singers need ten years' training before starting to look for any reward.

It is not easy to break into the operatic world; nevertheless I kept at it. With much hard work I became a freelance singer, which fitted in with having a family. It was a hectic life, and fraught with disappointments; fortunately, I had plenty of energy, and Leslie was very supportive.

Singing occupied some twenty years of my life, and I was very sad when I had to give it up. But that career is over, and I prefer not to look back. It is only relevant to my work now in that the training taught me to appreciate the value of discipline, and to be at ease on a platform when lecturing and taking seminars.

My back continued to be painful, and I often went off to sing with a bottle of Disprin in my pocket. I also suffered badly from pre-menstrual tension; one day, some twelve years after my marriage, I read in a booklet by Barbara Cartland that this could be relieved by taking calcium. I started taking bonemeal tablets, and was so impressed with the results that I began reading everything I could about vitamin and mineral therapy. This was well before the current interest in nutrition, and some of my friends thought me cranky. However, I studied the subject in depth and became quite an expert.

While I was developing this interest, I had to undergo a minor gynaecological operation during which my legs became locked almost over my head. When I was X-rayed in this agonizing position it was found that I had a ruptured disc pressing on the sciatic nerve. It was an enormous relief to know that my suffering had a physical cause!

I was offered surgery to end the pain, but it would have locked the vertebrae, making it impossible for me to bend, so I refused. I decided instead to cure myself with vitamin and mineral therapy and yoga. I was teaching myself yoga from a book by Indra Devi, a well-known Indian teacher, and the whole family used to join in. It gave Janet a good start; she now teaches yoga herself.

My back wasn't completely cured until some years later. I had been told that as I grew older the ruptured disc would shrivel and stop putting pressure on the nerve; when we went to live in a hot climate this speeded up this process. But I don't think my cure would have been so complete if I hadn't strengthened my spinal muscles with yoga and taken lots of vitamins. Meanwhile, it was only my ability to leave my body and find another dimension that enabled me to carry on.

Some inner urge was pushing me to investigate other aspects of health, and I also became fascinated by hand-reading. On my thirtieth birthday my children had given me a book on palmistry; it was the start of a sixteen-year study which led me into medical hand analysis. This is quite a fine art; I learned to take palm-prints, using printer's ink and a sheet of glass, in order to examine the tiny dots and breaks in the lines which reveal a person's health and nutritional status.

I began reading the hands of friends, relations and colleagues – everyone who called left our house with inky palms! I enjoyed it, and my knowledge of vitamin and mineral therapy enabled me to advise people on what supplements they needed. I found that I was able to help a lot of people with their problems, emotional as well as physical.

Some people regarded my palm-reading as 'the occult', but I always denied this strenuously. To me it was clearly quite scientific, and I never thought of myself as psychic. Yet throughout these years some strange things happened, of the kind known as psychic phenomena.

As soon as we had moved into our own home I noticed that objects were repeatedly being moved: I would put a watch down on a dressing-table and when I looked for it it would be gone. Then, when I looked again a little later, there it would be. I think many people have this experience without realizing it, because the obvious explanation is that one hasn't been looking properly! But this happened too often to be explained away so simply.

I also used to hear conversations going on in the street outside in the middle of the night – often gossipy conversations between two women. I used to jump out of bed in annoyance, but could see no one, and Leslie couldn't hear the voices at all. I don't think that these were ghosts; rather, that my mind was going back in time to tune into conversations that had happened some time before.

One night I dreamed that a friend of my mother, who had been in a coma for a year, came to tell me she had died. She gave me some specific instructions: everyone was to buy a separate wreath and not put their money towards one large one! At six o'clock next morning I rang my mother to tell her, apologizing for ringing so early. She replied: 'Don't worry. I heard about it an hour ago.' We had to laugh over the instructions: during her lifetime the lady had been constantly giving orders!

In those days I said very little about these experiences, except to Leslie who was forced to share them. I knew that people would think me odd; I also felt that they were special to me and that I wasn't meant to talk about them.

We had been married twenty years; the children were growing up, and I was totally occupied with singing, vitamin and mineral therapy, hand analysis and yoga. Then, from 1967 to 1969, we went through two incredibly difficult years, fraught with family problems and tragedies. I became very low-spirited and run-down, and when my mother died after a stroke I was so shaken that we decided to emigrate to Spain and begin a new life. Leslie had his own business by now, and planned to start one out there. I hated giving up my singing, but I was still suffering terribly with my back, especially in cold weather. There seemed to be nothing to keep us in England, and shortly after my mother's death we left for Spain.

Only after building ourselves a beautiful villa did we discover that it was impossible to get the necessary permits to start a business. Leslie had to return to England, while I stayed on to recover my health. I was out there for four years in all. Geoffrey was married, and Janet, now sixteen, left school and joined me in Spain, where she continued studying on her own and taught herself to type.

Gradually I recuperated from our recent troubles. I walked the hills with my dog and cat, absorbing nature and feeling at one with the earth and sky. Life was very basic and extremely hard, but the difficulties of daily living helped me to reconsider my values.

I continued to visit my other dimension. I always came back feeling more positive and with greater peace of mind, which helped me with the many decisions I had to take in Leslie's absence. The view from the villa was wonderful; it overlooked a great valley leading to the sea. Looking out over that vastness gave me the same kind of feeling that I had in the garden – a feeling of total peace and an uncluttered mind.

Something inside was compelling me to look beyond the visible world, and I spent hours gazing at the sky above the sea and at the stars at night. I started writing poetry and short stories for hours on end, which also brought me peace.

One afternoon Janet and I were lying on twin beds taking a siesta when something made me open my eyes. Standing at the foot of my bed, as real as she had been in life, was my mother. I called out to her, and she smiled. 'Janet!' I exclaimed. 'Nanny is here.'

Janet could see no one. She said: 'Don't be silly. Nanny's dead.'

My mother then left the room. I got up and followed her into the passage. It was empty. I ran from one room to another looking for her, but she had disappeared. I felt overwhelmed by loss.

My mother's appearance had been so solidly alive, I thought she had really returned from the dead. But why had she come back? What had she wanted to say? I felt sure she had been trying to tell me something, but couldn't fathom what.

About a month after my mother's visit I suddenly started to have choking attacks; for up to an hour I would find myself unable to breathe, while my heart palpitated wildly. It was extremely frightening, and Janet thought more than once that I was going to die.

I had only just begun to learn Spanish, and after some fruitless efforts I gave up trying to communicate my problem to the local doctors. I tried to ignore it, but the attacks continued. Since many doctors put strange symptoms down to a 'woman's age', I assumed that the cause must be 'my age' – which was forty-two. I could find no other explanation.

Janet and I became very close in Spain, and began to share experiences in a way we hadn't been able to do before. There was not much to do in the evenings, so to pass the time we practised projecting ourselves mentally to the nearest village. We'd take a look at what was going on there – which of our friends was in a particular café at a certain time, for instance. Next day we would check, and about eight times out of ten learned that we were right. We never connected this game with psychic abilities; it seemed perfectly logical to be able to extend our minds in this way.

In 1974, Janet and I returned to England. Our departure was overshadowed for me by having to put my cat and dog to sleep. It was a terrible decision to have to make; I had no right to take a life, and I was very close to them. But I knew they would never survive being parted from me in quarantine, and leaving them behind was out of the question. At least the local vet was a compassionate man; I had often taken sick strays to him to be put down in the English way – with an injection, rather than with arsenic as the Spanish custom was.

Afterwards the vet walked four hundred yards up the road to where I was sitting in the car, and held my hand. I couldn't speak; I just sat sobbing. Throughout the journey home I could think of nothing but the animals, and I grieved for them a long time. I was helped only by the thought that they had had more love than most pets get in a full lifetime.

Leslie had found us a flat in an old house while we looked around for more suitable accommodation. When we met our landlord, a vicar, he seemed very nervous and made a point of insisting that we should have no dealings with the occult. We assured him that we didn't indulge in that sort of thing and had no interest in it – which we hadn't. We were all too busy trying to reshape our lives.

However, the atmosphere was rather spooky, and some time after we had left that house I heard it had been exorcized. Some strange things happened while we were there. Once, when I was alone in the house, I left the water running for a bath. I returned to the bathroom five minutes later and found that the taps had been turned off. When I turned them on again, the water ran quite normally. Another time, we were all having a meal when we heard a loud crash from the bedroom. The door of the wardrobe had been lifted off its hinges and thrown against the wall; it took three of us to replace it. I laughed and said: 'Somebody's trying to tell us something!'

Janet was lying in bed one evening when she was frightened by hearing a man's voice speaking to her; then the bedroom door opened, although no one was there. Later, when she met her first husband, she recognized his voice as the one she had heard. The memory still sends chills up her spine.

My attacks of dizziness and choking were steadily getting worse, and were now accompanied by excruciating stomach pains. They frequently disrupted my life, and were alarming as well as painful. Once, when the palpitations were particularly frightening, my doctor arranged for me to have an electrocardiogram, but the results provided no explanation. I was beginning to feel quite desperate.

One evening I was lying down in the gathering darkness chatting to Janet. Suddenly she exclaimed: 'Look, there's a light!'

I followed her glance. In a corner of the room was a blue light, just like the one I'd seen when Harry Edwards had been sending me healing. It stayed there for about an hour without moving.

We watched it, fascinated. I had never told Janet about the first light, and she was very curious about it. I had no idea why it was there, but assumed that it meant there were spirit people around.

After a few months we moved to a flat in Sutton. It was vast, taking up two storeys and with no less than three halls. Our bedroom was like a ballroom! We were able to buy it very cheaply, which was extremely lucky as we had lost most of our money. The stress of running his own business had affected Leslie's health, and he began working as a minicab driver, which suited him much better. I had to work, too, despite my attacks. There was no way I could return to singing, so I took an office job.

During our three-year separation Leslie and I had inevitably grown apart; now it was clear that our marriage was under strain, which did not improve my health. I felt so ill that I became convinced I was going to die.

While travelling to work one day I was idly turning the pages of a book on hand analysis when I came across an advertisement for a well-known medium, Charles Horrey. Remembering that my grandmother could predict the future, I decided to find out whether my attacks were going to finish me off altogether. Scared at what he might tell me, I nevertheless felt impelled to make an appointment with him the following week. I had no idea that this meeting was to mark a complete turning-point in my life: that the attacks I had been suffering from had been caused by a build-up of unused energy; that I would be told that, far from dying, I was to live and heal others!

My sitting with Mr Horrey left me in a state of total confusion. I couldn't believe that I was a healer. Yet Mr Horrey had spoken with total conviction. I was in no doubt my mother had been communicating through him. I recalled her appearance in Spain, and the feeling that she had been trying to tell me something. Since my return, too, I had often been aware of her presence and had even heard her voice, reassuring me that everything was going to be all right.

Now Mr Horrey had said: 'Your mother is giving you something you always wanted, but in a different way.' She had known how upset I was when she had stopped me becoming a vet; perhaps she was trying to make amends by getting me to become a healer. Well, that was certainly different.

'You are already healing people,' Charles Horrey had said. I remembered all the people who had rung up after I'd analysed their hands and said: 'You know that vitamin you recommended? Well, I haven't got it yet, but I felt so much better after seeing you.' I had always assumed they felt better because they'd been able to talk to someone. Surely *that* wasn't healing?

When I got home I went straight into the kitchen where we sat in the evening, and told Leslie and Janet everything. They listened in silence, clearly fascinated.

Then Janet said: 'Trust Nanny to make you a second Harry Edwards!' Laughter brought us down to earth again. 'What will you have to do?' Janet asked.

'He just told me I would be taught, and when I asked by whom he said it will be automatic. He said thousands of people would be sent to me for healing.'

After recovering from the prospect of queues of people at our front door, Leslie said: 'Well, if getting rid of all this healing power will help you get better, perhaps you should do it.'

Leslie seemed to be accepting the situation; I was still in a state of shock and wonderment.

So far my experiences had been just that, my own private experiences; hand analysis had been a relatively light-hearted exercise. The idea of passing on messages to others and having people relying on me for healing became more ludicrous every time I thought about it. I decided to wait and see. After all, I had a living to earn.

I said to Leslie: 'There was something else. The medium told me he could see a white horse in a field and beside it a man. The man's name was Tom, and he said that Tom was asking me to forgive him.'

My husband laughed. 'Who on earth is Tom?'

'I haven't the faintest idea!'

For several days we tried in vain to work out Tom's identity. Later, the same message was repeated by two other mediums. Tom and the white horse became a running joke.

One reason I found it hard to accept that I was a healer was that I thought healers had to be 'holy', and I wasn't! From my days in the theatre I had acquired a rich vocabulary, and my sense of humour was pretty earthy. I was clearly quite unsuitable, and this really worried me. I was more ready to accept that I was psychic. It began to dawn on me that when reading people's hands I often found myself making accurate statements which were not based on the lines and dots I was studying so scientifically.

After talking with Leslie and Janet I went into my bedroom and sat quietly. I closed my eyes and said in my head: Look, I've got a terrible vocabulary, and I'm not at all holy, and if you don't think I'm the right person I think you should leave me alone and go off and find someone else.

Immediately I felt a great surge of power in the room, and a sense of spirit people being all around. Even the furniture seemed to move. I thought: This is ridiculous; they obviously don't care what I'm like!

That was the first of what was to be a positive onslaught

of psychic phenomena which was to continue for three months. It was as if, by accepting that I was a medium, I had released a mental block which allowed a tremendous, almost explosive, opening-up of my psyche.

I'd seen and heard spirit people all my life, but this was different. From then on, the whole place seemed to go mad. I saw spirit faces everywhere – faces of all kinds and nationalities, on walls, on the carpet, around the television set, coming and going, appearing and disappearing. I could hear people whispering and talking around me nearly all the time. Often this was accompanied by a kind of pulsating energy, which used to make me almost rattle. I didn't understand it at the time, but I know now that this was due to the power of the energy that had been built up in me.

A couple of days later I was chatting with a friend of ours who had been crippled with backache for over a year. I told him about my visit to Charles Horrey; he, too, thought that the idea of my becoming a healer was highly comic.

I said jokingly, 'Let me try on you!' and laid my hands on his back. Neither of us believed anything would happen. I asked if he could feel anything, and he said: 'No. But it feels good.' Then: 'Oh, I can feel some heat!'

'Can you? Can you really?' I grew quite excited, though I could feel nothing in my hands. 'Well, if you think it's worth it, I'll carry on.'

Then he said: 'Good Lord, it's getting hotter and hotter! Your hands are burning!'

When it felt like time to stop, I asked if he felt better, and he said: 'No!'

'Well, that was a waste of time!' I remarked. Obviously I had no talent as a healer.

When we next met two days later he said: 'Do you know, the pain in my back disappeared the next day and I haven't had it since!' I was more thrilled for him than for myself. Perhaps, after all, I could help others in this way.

I soon had an opportunity to try out my powers of mediumship, too.

Everyone in the office knew I read hands, and a director of a company which shared the same building, a man I'd never met before, asked me to give him a reading. I looked at his palm and heard myself telling him on no account to have anything to do with boats; it would be dangerous.

To my horror, the poor man literally had a fit! He slumped to the floor, knocking his head, and passed out cold. I just stood there, dumbstruck. When he'd been looked after, one of my colleagues told me that he was epileptic – and had just invested money in a small fishing fleet!

That evening I was telling Leslie this story when a lady arrived and introduced herself as the director's wife. I thought she'd come to berate me, and immediately started to apologize; I told her the incident had put me off hand-reading for ever.

'Oh, I do hope not,' she said. 'I've come to ask you to read mine!'

I had to refuse. There was no way I wanted a repeat performance that evening.

When I walked through the drawing office the next day, all the men were sitting at their desks with gloves on!

For a couple of weeks I tried to push out of my mind everything that Mr Horrey had told me. I was forty-six, I was working very hard, Janet was having problems which needed my attention, and I was already helping people in the evenings with hand analysis. I didn't see how I could find the time to be a healer, even if I had the ability – which I seriously doubted.

I was still resisting the idea. Healing simply wasn't me. Hand analysis was logical and scientific; all of this seemed illogical. I thought that a healer was a special sort of person possessed of some magical secret. I didn't feel at all special, and had no idea how healing was done. I used to look at seriously crippled people, and read about people

37

with cancer, and think: I couldn't do anything about that! It was a long time before I realized that it is not the healer who does the healing; that we are simply vehicles for healing energy, or life force, and that other minds are helping us.

However, encouraged by my success with my friend's back, I did offer to lay my hands on one or two friends with aches and pains. To my great surprise, they seemed to feel better. Despite myself, I was beginning my career as a healer. My life suddenly became extremely busy; in the evenings, after a day's work in London, I would be healing and giving sittings at home in Sutton.

The transition was far from easy. Phenomena continued to come thick and fast, sometimes frightening in their regularity and even ferocity. On a perfectly still night a wind would howl through our room; sometimes our bed would move. Leslie went out to sleep in the car at four o'clock one morning because he couldn't stand it. If I hadn't known I was psychic, I'd have been very worried. And any husband but Leslie would probably have taken me to see a psychiatrist!

Among the less enjoyable events was the time when I tried to turn over in bed one night and found I couldn't move. I seemed to be pinned in place by something as solid as a rock. I woke Leslie: as he put the light on I felt the 'rock' disappear. I know now that it was energy that had built up around me whilst I slept.

About two weeks after all this started I was at work in my office when I became aware that I was not alone. I looked up to see standing in front of me a man with a thoughtful face and a shaggy moustache. He was wearing a frock-coat and small metal glasses and was so obviously from another age that I realized immediately that he was a spirit. He wasn't a 'misty person': his top half looked quite solid, but he seemed to fade out from the frock-coat downwards!

It was the first time I had seen a spirit I didn't recognize, and I was fascinated. Telepathically my visitor conveyed to me that he had been a member of the London School of Medicine, and wanted to work with me. He also told me his name, but I was so surprised that I promptly forgot it.

I couldn't imagine how I could work with him, even if I wanted to, so I took in what he had to say without replying. Then he was gone. Well, that was interesting, I said to myself, and returned to my typing.

A few days later, I was in the office again when a voice told me to take up a pen. I found myself writing down further information about the doctor. He had specialized in arthritic conditions and heart complaints and wanted to help people through me. I couldn't understand how he could do this, or why he had picked on me. At home I told Leslie about this visitation. I said: 'What the hell does he mean? How on earth can I heal people with arthritis?' I still had no idea how healing worked. I put the doctor out of my mind.

Meanwhile the phenomena continued, some of them thoroughly enjoyable. I had never had any artistic talent, yet suddenly at work one day I found myself producing rather good drawings of faces. Unfortunately, this gift only lasted a couple of weeks – I had had visions of becoming an artist. It seems that this kind of thing occurs during the development of many psychics. It is as if you are being put through a training course and tried out at different skills. The ones that suit you you are allowed to keep! Evidently, I hadn't passed the drawing test.

I was quite open with my friends about what was going on, and they got used to being greeted with: 'You'll never guess what's happened now.' Only one suggested that I should see a psychiatrist, which I found hurtful; whatever was going on, I always had my feet firmly planted on the ground. But people are frightened of the unknown. Later on, some of my friends, to whom I gave a lot of clairvoyance and healing, talked about me to people who didn't know me, and were ridiculed for it. This bothered them so much that they didn't contact me for some time.

Although I was hurt, I knew that like so many people they needed time to come to terms with the existence of the paranormal.

There were bumps and thumps in the flat, and my bed used to move of its own accord. Objects disappeared and reappeared without rhyme or reason. Before the telephone rang I would hear it ring in my head and know that there would be a telephone call within minutes. Spirit people were appearing continuously, similar to the misty people I had seen while I was an evacuee, which I found a kind of comfort. I also heard voices trying to communicate with me all the time; the information they gave me was always for others, never for me.

Almost daily I would see a beam of light in the hall (not unlike the teleportation device in 'Star Trek'). Within this would appear people dressed in robes; I found them beautiful rather than frightening, and their presence usually heralded yet another fascinating new experience. In this world of both real and misty people it was difficult to take in the magnitude of what was happening.

I decided to see Charles Horrey again for guidance. He reassured me that these kinds of thing can happen to anybody who is a true medium. He also said that the phenomena would continue until I was absolutely convinced of the powers that were being channelled through me.

'You may not like them now,' he added, 'but when they stop you will miss them. You are going through the most exciting time in your mediumship. Enjoy it.'

He went on: 'I understand you've started healing?'

I said: 'Yes, but I still don't understand it. I don't know what I'm supposed to be doing.'

Mr Horrey repeated that I was already healing and was being taught; I should not go to any development groups as I could rely on my own experience. Then he began speaking about a doctor who wanted to work through me. 'I'm being told that you have had information about this doctor before,' he said, 'that he has contacted you. Have you been to see another medium?'

I said: 'I've never been to any medium except you.'

'That's very strange, because he is insistent that he has already been in contact with you.'

Suddenly I remembered the doctor who had manifested in my office. I really had forgotten about him.

'Oh, that's what he means!' said Charles Horrey. 'He's actually appeared to you! You must carry on working as a healer. Doctor Watson was a specialist in arthritic complaints, and you will have the ability to cure arthritis.'

I had to make an effort not to laugh. I thought: What on earth could I do with arthritis that the doctors can't achieve?

My doctor friend visited me twice more soon afterwards. Some of my hand-analysis clients used to tell me that they felt better when they listened to my voice, and if they needed help I would talk to them on the phone. During two of these calls, the doctor appeared and stood by the telephone during the conversation.

I visited Charles Horrey four times in all. On my fourth visit, he said: 'How many times do I have to tell you I cannot teach you anything? Go away, and work!' I was not to see him again for thirteen years.

As soon as I began to heal regularly my health improved. Once I allowed the energy to flow, my choking fits stopped and I felt on top of the world. (I still have to be careful not to get a build-up of energy, since it flows through me all the time; if I stop healing for a while for any reason, I go round healing my plants and my dogs.) I know now that it can take at least twelve hours for the energy to be absorbed by the patient's body and used for whatever purpose it is needed; that was why my friend's back wasn't cured immediately. Now all the energy I had been blocking over the last seven years was unleashed, and people felt the benefits very quickly.

Although our marriage was approaching its natural end – for one thing we were both so busy we hardly saw each other – in my healing work Leslie backed me all the way.

Just as Charles Horrey had predicted, all sorts of people began ringing for appointments, all by word of mouth. Leslie was responsible for many of them: people would get into his taxi complaining about their aches and pains, and he would say: 'Go and see my wife!' Pleased patients told their friends; people even began ringing from abroad asking for absent healing. It was quite extraordinary. Equally extraordinary was the fact that they were getting better!

Although I was healing successfully from the start, my mind was in a turmoil when I tried to work it all out. I still thought that healing was some form of magnetic energy from myself, and not from any other source. I carried out my own investigations over about two months and was convinced I was right, until a patient told me that when she had gone to bed she had felt hands on her chest and had gone to sleep very quickly, and another told me that someone had drawn the curtains while she was in bed. Well, that certainly didn't tie in with my theories.

I had accepted by this time that I was in communication with another dimension. But – I really don't know why – I was reluctant to believe that it was an outside force that produced the healing energies, or to accept that doctors who had died were working through me.

How did they work through me? Why was this energy channelled through one person and not through another? I didn't want to feel that someone else was in control of me, and kept constructing my own theories, only to have them proved wrong. I think this is actually the best way to learn! Having to acknowledge you are wrong shakes up your preconceived ideas and makes you think.

Against Charles Horrey's advice, I did go twice with a friend to a development group run by a spiritualist medium, but I giggled so much I couldn't go back! Everything was taken so seriously, and I couldn't believe that things were as complicated as was made out. My friend said she was glad when I left the group, so that she could concentrate on what was being said!

Mr Horrey was right again. It has always been very

important for me to find things out for myself, and ever since then I have stayed away from groups. But there were so many things I wanted to know! My curiosity at last got the better of me, and I visited a psychic bookshop in London. Perhaps I could help myself without clouding my mind too much.

It was difficult to choose among the quantities of books on healing, mediumship, and evidence of survival after death. I wondered why this information was not available in general bookshops. It saddened me that the world at large was ignorant of so many remarkable facts because people weren't being offered the choice of reading.

Over the next few years I read everything I could. I rejected quite a lot, but there was enough sensible information to help me understand what was happening. Another way in which I learned was through the information that I was given to pass on. I would find myself relaying spiritual messages that made sense to me as well as to the recipients.

It is clear – and other mediums confirm this – that people like me are chosen to do our work. I've often been asked who does the choosing, and I always answer: 'I wish I knew! Because I'd like to have a few words with him!' I was often aware, however, that certain people were training me, particularly when I was healing, including the doctor who had first made contact with me. I saw a lot of him during these early days, and began to be able to communicate with him telepathically. One day I conveyed to him my anxiety that my earthy language made me unsuitable to be a healer.

The message I got back was: 'Betty, if you'd ever heard a surgeon talking while he's operating, or doctors talking among themselves, you'd know their language is abominable!'

So perhaps they thought they'd got the right woman! I must hasten to add that since I've been healing my 'language' has automatically been toned down.

Other spirits arrived, wanting to work with me. Two of them I have hesitated to write about, because I realize that the stories sound so incredible.

There was a phase when I began seeing rather frightening pictures of snakes, and found myself writing a lot of poetry. I was in bed one night when a man appeared and said: 'I'm William Blake, and I'd like to work with you.' It was he who was sending me these drawings.

At that time I had no idea who he was. All I knew was that I thought his pictures were creepy. I said: 'Please go away. I don't want this.' When a friend told me that Blake was a famous mystical artist and poet I went to the library to find out more about him, and saw drawings exactly like those he had been sending me.

After about two weeks of being shown these terrifying pictures, I finally said to him: 'Look, will you please push off!' I never saw him again.

Soon afterwards a little man arrived, very French-looking with a beard. He told me he was Louis Pasteur; he, too, wanted to work through me. I *had* heard of Pasteur, but couldn't believe that someone so eminent would want to work through me. He came three times before I was convinced. I ought perhaps to have told him I'd be delighted to work with him. But I wasn't really delighted; I was rather overwhelmed and wondered why he'd chosen me. However, I didn't tell him to go away, either, and I can only say that each day brought the most incredible healings. I had never seen Pasteur's portrait; out of interest I looked him up in the library, too, and was fascinated to find that he looked exactly like his picture.

Until now, I've never mentioned these visitors to anyone except my family, because I feel rather embarrassed about it. I myself am very suspicious when mediums talk about contacting the spirits of famous people; it's a world in which it's all too easy to name-drop! But I can only say that it happened.

New phenomena kept occurring. One morning when I

awoke I was astonished to see a large eye looking at me from the ceiling above my bed. It was about the size of a dinner-plate, complete with eyelids. Intrigued, I stared back. It was a kindly eye and it gave me a tremendous feeling of peace. It was so real that I pointed it out to Leslie, but he couldn't see it.

This eye followed me everywhere I went. It appeared on walls, carpets and furniture, even on the floor; practically everywhere I looked the eye would be looking back at me. Like all the other phenomena, I became accustomed to having it around.

About nine months later I was looking in the mirror when I suddenly saw that the eye was identical with my own; I realized that this was the third eye that I had read about, and that what I was experiencing was its opening. I had never before accepted that we have a third eye, but there it was. My eye and I lived happily together for another two or three years and then it disappeared. I missed it; I always found it a great comfort.

At about the time the eye first appeared, I began to see auras. The first time this happened was a magical experience. We had a cage-bird, a cross between a linnet and a roller canary, which we used to let free to fly around the bedroom. It would sing so loudly that Janet, who is also a musician, couldn't hear herself playing her guitar!

One day while the bird was sitting in the window singing I saw the most beautiful blue light glowing around it. When it stopped singing this light seemed to be contained within what looked like a pencil outline close to its body; then when it began to sing again the blue aura expanded to about half an inch all around. It was very beautiful and quite awe-inspiring. I have seen many thousands of auras since then, but that one made the most impact on my senses.

Soon after seeing the aura around the bird, I began to see auras around people; as time went on I learned to interpret their colours. I also began to see – as if someone were showing them to me – what looked like tubes running through people. I became aware that, where there was a blockage in a tube, that was the area where I should put my hands, regardless of where the pain was felt. Later, through my reading, I realized that these tubes corresponded with the meridian lines of Chinese acupuncture.

After the first three months the phenomena stopped being so violent and unexpected, though they have continued in various forms to this day. I was healing regularly, and by now I was enjoying it very much. As Mr Horrey had foretold, most of my early patients had arthritic problems. Then, after two years, there were six months during which I had a spate of patients with Menière's disease, followed by three months of people with visual problems.

I was clearly being trained and tested. How this training takes place is very interesting. Some healers stop at one problem and become specialists in that; in my case I seem to have passed the whole course, because I now get patients with every problem under the sun.

Over the next few years I was to see hundreds of cases, some of them very severe. People came who had given up all hope of ever using their limbs fully again; almost all were able to return to normal activity. As time went by, the time it took to heal them became shorter; quite often it was instantaneous.

Practically everyone could feel a tremendous heat or tingling going through their bodies, and I could feel vibrations going through them; sometimes the couch seemed to vibrate as well. My hands were automatically guided to the part of the body that needed healing, regardless of the location of the pain.

During healing I would be given information to pass on to my patients, about relations who were dead, and about the future. I remember one woman with a frozen shoulder who used to write down all this information and date her notes. Her husband was very sceptical, and she was determined to prove him wrong if it killed her! When something happened that had been predicted she used to get her notes and show them to him. Then she'd ring me up and say: 'I told him so!' When her shoulder was completely cured he had to be convinced of that at least, and eventually came for healing himself.

Everyone who came for healing became a friend. Whole families came to me, and many of them treated me as their family doctor. I was extremely careful not to interfere with the relationship they had with their GP, but sometimes it was difficult to remain neutral. Most of them were tired of their doctor's negative attitude and with taking drugs which simply suppressed their symptoms. People want to be cured!

Several phenomena occurred during the healing sessions themselves. One I thoroughly disliked was the smell of ether which manifested every time I started healing. At first I thought it might be coming from outside the house, but it soon became apparent that it was emanating from somewhere in the healing-room. This manifestation lasted over a period of three years. It was unpleasant to live with as the smell pervaded the flat long after I had finished healing for the day. I asked the advice of another medium, who said it was sent to encourage me. I hated it! However, it gave patients an enormous amount of confidence, since they realized that something special was happening.

On many occasions, too, a cold wind would blow through my healing-room. The flat was always very warm, and totally draught-proof, yet even on a summer's day I'd have to put a gas-fire on. This is quite a common experience among healers; I believe it is due to the presence of a number of spirits, which draw on the heat.

Another uncanny phenomenon was a sensation like strands of spider's web on my face and on those of people I was healing; I would see them trying to remove it from their face and hands. The only explanation I have for this is that these were some sort of strands of energy floating around.

There was also a number of times when I became invisible to the person I was healing. After I had finished they would say, 'You disappeared!' although I had felt nothing unusual. I have come to the conclusion that this was an effect of the massive amount of energy around me at the time. It would become so dense that it would actually screen me from view in a kind of blue mist.

During my years of training I could feel my mother's presence all the time. In Sutton, whenever I relaxed in my favourite armchair, I would feel her hand gently touch my shoulder; it was very comforting. I told Leslie and many friends but I never mentioned it to Janet, because I thought it would make her nervous.

One evening, after I'd been healing for about two years, Leslie and I went out to a party leaving Janet alone with our Dobermann bitch, Lady. We returned at half-past midnight to find that Janet had spent the evening locked in her attic bedroom with the dog, quite terrified. While she was watching television in my armchair, a hand had been placed on her shoulder. I told her not to worry, it was only Nanny, and it happened to me every evening. 'Why the hell didn't you tell me?' said Janet.

This brought home to me the fact that Janet was very psychic, and I began confiding in her more about my own experiences.

My mother contacted me in every way she could. Whenever I went to a spiritualist meeting she would always be up front! It makes me laugh to think that my mother, who wouldn't have been caught dead at a spiritualist meeting in her lifetime, haunted the ones I went to after her death!

Janet used to accompany me to these meetings, although she didn't really approve of my going and felt I didn't belong there. I had no desire to become a spiritualist, or any other kind of 'ist'; but I was still learning, and was interested to see how other people worked. I was often disappointed that public demonstrations of mediumship and clairvoyance came over as a kind of music-hall act, and very glad that I didn't have to be a platform medium.

One or two mediums, however, impressed me by their

intelligence. It was one of these who gave me a further message from the mysterious Tom with the white horse. I still had no idea who he was. The mystery was solved at last when I caught a very bad flu virus, during which I left my body several times. Opening my eyes at one stage, I saw a white-haired man standing at the foot of the bed. He said: 'Betty, please forgive me. I could have helped you and I didn't. It was cowardly.'

I couldn't believe it. He was the husband of the awful woman I had been billeted with as an evacuee – and of course his name was Tom! I put my hand out to him, but he had gone. And now I remembered the white horse, which used to be in a field opposite the house. Tom was a nice man, and I had always felt terribly sorry for him even as a child.

From that moment I began to recover from my flu. Tom had obviously been healing me.

In 1982 I had been healing for seven years. Four years earlier I had given up my job to heal full-time and I was healing all hours of the day. It was hard work, but I loved helping people, and was pushed on by the thrill of seeing people get better, after suffering so much myself.

My private life was less happy, however, and Leslie and I had just agreed to separate when he became seriously ill. He had had worrying symptoms for some time but hadn't had them investigated, possibly frightened of what the doctors might tell him. While I was in Spain he and our son Geoffrey made a hang-glider, and when they tried it out he had an accident and damaged his shoulder; this old injury gave me an opportunity to give him masses of healing.

Now it turned out that he had cancer of the intestine, requiring a major operation. Fortunately, although the growth was definitely malignant and the doctors said he had had it for years, it was not of the worst kind; I feel this must be because of all the healing he had been given.

Just before he came home to convalesce, some tubes

which had been inserted in his stomach were removed. Two days later one of the wounds split wide open, and we hastily called the surgeon. He said that this was not uncommon, and that it would take six weeks to heal. He couldn't stitch the wound because the flesh round it was too thin and tender, and we had to dress it with pads from the chemist.

I gave Leslie a lot of healing that day. He was sleeping in a single bed beside mine; all of a sudden in the middle of the night he woke me up, exclaiming: 'Jesus, what's happening to me? Look at my arms and legs. I can't control them!' I looked, and his arms and legs were moving around all over the place.

I knew what was happening, because some of my patients had had similar experiences. I said: 'Oh, that's good. You'll be better in the morning. You're being given some wonderful healing!'

'I bloody well hope so,' said Leslie.

When we went to change his dressing in the morning the wound had completely healed. We called the surgeon, and after he had examined him I told him that I was a healer and had given Leslie an hour's healing the previous evening.

The surgeon took this information calmly. He said to Leslie: 'All I can say is, you are a very lucky man to have a wife like that!'

Leslie went on to make a rapid recovery, and has never had to have any post-operative treatment; I'm glad to report that he is still completely well.

When Leslie was completely better we parted company; it was an amicable separation, and we are still friends. Even so, I went through quite a bad patch emotionally and felt very lonely.

One day the phone rang. When I answered it a woman's voice said: 'Hallo, Betty.' It sounded familiar, but I couldn't immediately place it; I asked who it was.

'It's Mum,' she said.

Before I could speak, she went on: 'We are so pleased

for you. We've been watching everything you've been doing, and we are all helping you.'

Feeling amazingly calm, I asked who 'all' was, and she said: 'All of us.'

'Who are "all"?'

She said: 'Dad's helping you, and Gwen, and Elizabeth.' It was the mention of Gwen, a friend who had sometimes looked after me as a child, which convinced me this could be no one but my mother.

She went on: 'Wonderful things are going to happen for you. It is no coincidence that you have been chosen to do this work. We know far more now than we did. You were chosen, a long time ago. I know so much now.'

From what she said, I understood that she was actively involved in helping me. She asked me to tell Janet, who was also having problems, that she was helping her and looking after her. Janet always feels my mother around, even more than I do now.

We talked for about ten minutes, during which she told me about amazing things that were going to happen to me. I just kept saying, 'Are you all right, Mum? Are you sure you're all right?' as though she'd been away on a long journey, but I didn't even feel surprised. It was as if I was transported into another, but perfectly real, world. When I put the phone down, however, I found myself in a state of shock. Had it really happened?

When I told Janet I said: 'Don't tell anyone else. People will really think I've flipped this time!'

Recently, I have told one or two people, and they always want to know whether my mother had to dial our number! It's true that spirit people make a lot of use of electricity, but I've no idea at what point they break into the telephone system!

Three months later I was browsing in a bookshop and there in front of me was a book called *Phone Calls from the Dead*. I bought it, and couldn't wait to get home to read it. I was amazed to find that others had had the same experience, including perfectly ordinary people as well as mediums. Reading this made me feel less alone. But when I recall that conversation I am still filled with a sense of the miraculous.

I stayed on in the huge Sutton flat, and for the first time had to deal with paying bills and the mortgage. It wasn't at all easy, and I worked very hard. People would telephone me for guidance from six in the morning till one o'clock the next. Some just turned up on the doorstep; others telephoned from abroad in the middle of the night asking for clairvoyance and healing.

It was a mad life, but there was some phenomenal healing going on! I was also supported in some incredible ways. I often worked late into the evening; I would put my supper to cook in the pressure cooker and then, totally absorbed in my healing, forget about it. The gas would always be turned off at the right time, and the food would be perfectly cooked.

Soon after Leslie left a bill arrived for £85, which I couldn't pay, and I was extremely worried about it. I am an avid reader; when I next opened the book I was reading, there was a five-pound note. I thought I must have left it in the book myself; but that week, every time I took a book from a shelf, no matter at what page I opened it, there would be another five-pound note!

I found this as incredible as my mother's telephone call. The notes continued arriving until I had acquired £80. Then they stopped for two days. Then, after doing some spring cleaning, I went to the front door to greet a patient and there, on the mat, where I had just been vacuuming, was a five-pound note, making up the £85 I needed.

I have never received any more money in that way and certainly don't expect to do so. Funnily enough, another phenomenon worked in quite the reverse way. Shortly after this I was asked to attend a seminar in Segovia and before I left I bought sixteen pairs of stockings to make sure I didn't run out while I was abroad. I put them in a drawer until the time came to pack; when I opened it every single pair had vanished. I just hope that whoever received my stockings needed them more than I did!

Though we kept in touch, Leslie was no longer my husband. Some other close friendships had broken up for various reasons, much of the past had been washed away, and I was very alone. I felt rather depressed, and very sad.

At this point, Michael and Clementina Bentine came into my life. An acquaintance told him that I was in a distressed state, and asked him to ring me.

So out of the blue one day Michael rang me, saying: 'I understand you're in trouble.' I was amazed. Michael has had many tragedies of his own, and is a very busy man; I thought it was quite lovely that he should think about helping a complete stranger. After we had talked for a while I felt my sadness lifting for the first time for ages. Then I said: 'Excuse me, but I think your wife is in trouble.'

I diagnosed, correctly, that she had a frozen shoulder, and I heard Michael call out: 'Clem, you must come and hear this!' He asked if he could bring her for healing, and of course I said yes. Although she had been to all sorts of therapists, her shoulder was completely cured after one healing, which was nice – she told everyone she'd had a miracle cure!

The Bentines were wonderful to me; they used to pick me up at weekends and take me to their home. We became very good friends, and I became hooked on Clementina's cooking!

Michael is very psychic. In November 1983 he told me: 'The man you are going to share the rest of your life with will be living with you before I return from America next May.' He added: 'It's someone you know already.'

I said: 'Michael, anyone I already know – forget it!'

He smiled and said: 'Wait and see. You'll be living in a cottage in the country.'

Some time before I had given a sitting to a businessman. He had been back several times; I liked him, but would never in my wildest dreams have thought of Alan as a suitor. I hadn't seen him for six months when he suddenly got in touch with me, this time to offer *me* help; he felt he owed me a lot since the clairvoyance I had given him had been extremely useful. I met Alan for lunch, and by the following March we were living together.

When Michael returned to this country in May, he and Clementina invited us for lunch. When he opened the door to us Michael said: 'That's him! That's the man I saw!'

Alan said: 'Thank God for that!'

After we moved into our current home – in the country, just as Michael predicted – all kinds of phenomena started up again! Objects disappeared and reappeared again, and there have been one or two other odd happenings. Alan has taken it all in his stride. He has also put a stop to my working all hours of the day and night, and encouraged me to write this book; without his support I could not have written it.

I have now been working as a healer and medium for thirteen years. I have never advertised or sought publicity, but as I have become better-known I have been asked to give lectures and teach. I have taught in schools – I have a particular empathy with teenagers – and have taken many seminars abroad.

Now I have the opportunity to do what I have been wanting to do for a long time: to write this book so that my message will reach a wider public. It is a message about healing, about mediumship, about the survival of the mind after death, and about the most amazing phenomenon of all – which I call *mind energy*.

PART ONE

Spiritual Gifts

ONE

Mind Energy

> Mind no longer appears as an accidental intruder into
> the realm of matter: we are beginning to suspect that
> we ought rather to hail it as the 'Creator and governor
> of the realm of matter'.
>
> SIR JAMES JEANS, astronomer

Healing is the most wonderful form of complementary
medicine you can have.

To many people healing is a mystery, a combination of
mysticism, religious faith and the miraculous. If there is a
mystery, it is only because people choose to make it so:
there are logical explanations for most things if one cares
to look into them. Healing is simply the transmission of
life force, the energy that sustains every form of life.

Human beings are first and foremost energy beings.
Everyone has an energy counterpart which both occupies
the body and extends beyond it as the aura: it is this which
supplies life, health and vitality to the physical body.
When the energy system breaks down or is blocked in any
way, related parts of the body cease to vibrate with life
force, and this creates ill-health in the physical system.

Although there are still some sceptics, the concepts
of the life force and the energy system are becoming
increasingly accepted today. Many of the alternative or
complementary methods of healing, such as acupuncture,
have been based on these principles for centuries, and
those of us who constantly use and work with energy
experience 'miracles' every minute of every day. I believe
that a full understanding of these energies could revol-
utionize our attitudes to life.

We are surrounded by unseen forces, and although most people are unable to see them they can still feel them. When a breeze blows against your hair and face you cannot see it but you know it's there. When you receive an electric shock you cannot see it but you certainly know it's there! We accept facts and figures on trust from scientists and doctors about the workings of our bodies because we know them to be experts. If only the same approach could be taken to psychics and healers who can see and feel the energy system!

My own understanding of energy started from the time, thirteen years ago, when I saw the wonderful blue aura around our songbird, expanding as it sang, after which I could see auras around everyone. It was fascinating. The colours were all different, and I began to realize that every disability has its own radiation and colours. I began to understand, too, that there is a source of cosmic or universal energy, on which mind and body energy are dependent.

Healers have an extra supply of this life force, which can be used for the benefit of others; in a healing session it is automatically and naturally transmitted through the healer to the patient, usually by laying hands on them, though a number of other methods can also be used. As the energy flows to the patient, it is replenished from the never-ending supply of cosmic energy all around.

Once I understood that I had access to an extra supply of life force, I had fun experimenting with what that energy could do. One day, I practised for six whole hours trying to turn water into wine! (I only achieved a hint of pink, but I drank it anyway.) Now I reserve my energy for healing, but I have described some of my experiments in the last section of this book, so you can test your own energies.

What I believe to be my most important realization of all, however, occurred when I had been healing for about a year. This was the discovery of the energy round the head, which is separate and totally different from the aura.

One day a lady came to see me for help with a 'woman's complaint'. When I opened the door to her, I was surprised to see a mist around her head. When I looked more closely, I could see that its centre had a funnel-like appearance, as though it was being drawn inward and down into the body. I was so struck by this that as I showed her in I couldn't take my eyes off it; my visitor must have wondered why I was looking at her so intently.

While healing her, I could also see that the area around her brain was congested with this obviously negative energy. It occurred to me that with so much pressure there she must be having mental problems, and I asked her if she was suffering from depression. 'Yes,' she said, 'that's really why I came to see you.' The complaint she had told me about on arrival was a result of her depression.

I have always recognized the importance of positive thinking, and had already written some notes on the subject. I gave these to her to use at home, and in addition to receiving healing she worked at acquiring a new, positive attitude. This helped her considerably. Several healings later, the funnel-like appearance over her head had gone, and the energy was a complete circle radiating outwards.

That experience made a great impact on me, and I began studying the energy around the heads of everyone who came to me, and of people everywhere – in trains, buses, crowds – wherever I went. It was only after looking at thousands of people in all sorts of circumstances that I came to call this energy 'mind energy'.

I am convinced that recognizing the importance of mind energy could change people's attitudes to negativity and positivity the world over. I have seen so clearly the effects of thought on people's physical energy and health: how positive thinking stimulates it, causing the energy to expand outwards, while negativity draws that same energy downwards, eventually causing congestion throughout the body.

Everyone who is depressed has the same appearance. It always looks as if the energy is being drawn down in a funnel shape, through the top of the head and down into the body. In every case I can see how depression and negative thinking come to create an unnatural pressure on the brain, literally depressing and compressing it. I see, too, how this affects the electro-magnetic field around the head and that if it continues unchecked it eventually causes congestion in the energy counterpart and alters the body's biochemistry.

Yet in only twenty minutes passing an even greater energy through the body with healing can dislodge the compression and reverse the direction of the mind energy, enabling both mind and body to begin to heal.

In a healthy positive person the energy pulsating around the head is quite amazing. It surrounds the head as far as just below the ear, and is separate from the aura around the body. It can extend outwards *ad infinitum*, unlimited by space. The ability to see this has brought new meaning to the concepts of 'open'- and 'closed'-mindedness. In an open-minded person the expansion of the energy can be tremendous, whereas closed-minded people literally draw their minds in so that not only are they unreceptive to new ideas but they have also cut themselves off from the ability to attune to other people and even to nature.

Mind energy stimulates the physical functions of the brain, and it is fascinating to watch it expand and contract as someone is thinking. The brain itself is a 'junction-box' for the mind. In *Seance to Science*, Meek and Harris write that Dr Wilder Penfield, one of the first brain researchers to begin to raise questions about mind-brain connections, has permanently removed massive segments of a patient's brain, but still the 'mind' seemed to carry on as before without disturbance of consciousness. Similar findings have been shown on a television programme on the same subject, in which a woman's mind was found to be normal, though 85 per cent of her brain was 'inactive'. A superb illustration of the power of the mind is Christopher Nolan, the young man who recently won the Whitbread Book of the Year prize. Despite a damaged brain, he has enabled his powerful, intelligent and talented *mind* to fly free, unhampered by physical limitations.

When I first recognized the significance of mind energy I was tremendously excited. If positivity could reverse the energy, bringing about such incredible changes, then this was the secret of a healthy successful existence; this was the key which we all hold to our own destiny. I encouraged people even more strongly to get rid of, or at least control, negativity. In those who persevered the change was astonishing: their mind energy became bright and expansive, positively vibrating.

Mediums have always been able to 'see' the energy fields around the body; with the increased recognition of Kirlian photography, which shows these fields on film, they are beginning to be taken seriously. Perhaps in the future mind energy will also be captured in this way. After all, it has already been captured in art.

When I had been studying mind energy for some time, I walked into a church one day on impulse. Inside, I found myself looking at a painting of Christ, and at the halo round His head. There were some paintings of the saints, with their haloes; I looked at these, too, in astonishment.

It was quite shattering. Like everyone, I'd seen pictures of haloes all my life without thinking about them. Only at that moment did it dawn on me that they were identical with the energy I had been studying. Although most human beings have lost this faculty, I believe that the first illustrations of haloes were made by artists who had the ability to *see* the radiant energy of the mind.

My understanding of mind energy inevitably influences my diagnosis. Clairvoyant diagnosis is not the same as a medical diagnosis. It is the ability to diagnose the state of the patient's energy counterpart, where the physical problems begin; in fact I can see physical problems showing up in the energy field at least two years before they manifest in the body. And of course the state of the person's mind energy strongly affects the state of his energy counterpart, and must therefore be included in my assessment.

In clairvoyant diagnosis, I view the energy field around the body (the aura), the energy channels flowing through it, and the chakras or energy centres going down the body. I can also see the parts of the body which are under stress, as the energy counterpart occupies the body, taking the shape of the organs.

The aura is often described as having seven layers; I see only three, but for diagnosis this is quite enough. The very specific aura immediately round the body, which some people refer to as the etheric, is the one I use the most. Its colours are constantly changing as people's thoughts and states of health change; but there are definite patterns relating to particular conditions, and by constant observation I have learned how particular physical problems show up in the energy counterpart.

I get an overall picture when people first arrive. For example, if someone arrives after a recent quarrel the aura will be shot with red, mainly in the mind energy, although red streaks will also appear in the body aura. In someone with nerve problems, the first thing I will see in the aura is a kind of dirty green. In arthritis the aura contains a dull yellow shade; some people come complaining of rheumatism or arthritis, but when I view them I see not this dull yellow but a bright mauve. This shows that the problem is not arthritis, but stress, causing overactive adrenal glands and producing too much acid in the system. Bright mauve is a very common colour!

The auras of cancer patients often contain a lot of dark lifeless-looking patches. Dark areas appear in the body, too, where an organ has been removed; the energy still takes the shape of that organ but is much duller. When I see this, I check whether the person has had an operation; sometimes they haven't, and I then need to find out what that dull patch indicates, so that I can deal with it.

Also within the body, I can see the energy channels which correspond with the meridian lines of acupuncture and shiatsu; I believe the meridians were discovered in ancient China by people with clairvoyant sight. To me they appear as narrow whitish-yellow tubes. When I see an almost colourless section, diminished in circumference, I know there is a blockage in this area of the meridian preventing the free flow of energy; during the healing session I will work to release this.

Then there are the chakras, which some people refer to as energy centres. These are seven vortices in the energy system which draw in the life force from the limitless supply of cosmic energy in the universe, and control its flow through the body. They occupy approximately the same areas as some of the most important organs and glands of the body.

There are a number of books on yoga and on the chakras themselves which describe and illustrate this system. If you want to study this subject further, some I can recommend are listed at the end of the book. You may find that books vary in their descriptions of the colours, positions and functions of the chakras. This is not to say that anybody is 'wrong'; it is simply that people's perceptions differ.

I see seven main chakras, never more than two at a time, according to which part of the body I am working on. Going down the body, they are positioned at the top of the head, the forehead, the throat, the heart (in the centre over the breastbone), and over the spleen, just below the ribs on the left-hand side. Then there is the solar plexus chakra over the navel, and the important one at the base of the spine which is the seat of what is known as kundalini energy. In addition to these seven I see a very small one over the gall-bladder.

The chakras look like whirls of moving energy, roughly circular in shape although the one at the brow, relating to the third-eye area, is oval. They each contain predominant colours, and any change in the usual colour will indicate

63

that something is wrong. During healing, I concentrate on the energy fields until the colours have returned to normal.

I'm told that my perception of these colours differs from some traditional accounts. I honestly don't think this is important: if you show the same colour to ten different people, they will describe it in ten different ways. It's possible that every medium has his or her slightly differing method of diagnosis and set of colours. What is important is to experience things for oneself, and be true to that experience, rather than parroting other people's ideas. (So if your experience is different from what you read in books stay with your own unique thought.)

At their centres, the chakras are like whirlpools, constantly drawing in the life force or cosmic energy all around us in order to support the energy counterpart. When people are ill one or two chakras are likely to be under-energized, and these will need attention while I am healing. Sometimes chakras become *too* energized, because while they automatically draw in energy they don't automatically discharge it. In these cases the vortices look like tangled balls of wool.

Any disruption in the energy system will cause a problem in the physical body, which is the province of medical diagnosis. When a new patient comes I like to have their medical history and diagnosis before I scan the body to see how far it coincides with what I see. It's surprising how often it differs – not because doctors are necessarily wrong, but because conventional medicine doesn't take the energy system into account.

Very often the outward symptoms of an illness appear in quite a different area from the site of congested energy; clairvoyant diagnosis therefore complements medical diagnosis. Everyone I have given healing to has had his or her energy system blocked in some way or another. The advantage of healing is that a healer with clairvoyant sight can transfer energy directly into the congested area, and can cure or relieve so-called incurable complaints by clearing the blockages and revitalizing the energy.

The transference of energy opens up the energy channels in the patient's body, which uses it for whatever purpose it needs it. It can take twelve hours for results to be noticed, while the energy works through the system. This is the first step to a cure; when it is revitalized in this way, the patient's body heals itself. Although I sometimes speak about 'curing' this or that disease, I view the whole of life first and foremost in terms of energy, so it is more accurate to say that the congested energy causing the physical ailment has been removed. I also recommend healing as a preventative. If the energy system is revitalized three or four times a year to keep all the energy channels open, it should be possible to maintain optimum health.

Most people assume that healing energy comes from the healer's hands. In my experience healers draw in and radiate energy out from all their chakras, but especially from the chakra in the navel area. I have tried standing behind someone with my own hands behind my back; the person will still experience enormous heat in their lower back. During a healing session, however, I use my hands as a channel, and most people experience heat or tingling coming from them. In addition my mind energy links up with the patient's mind energy; experiments have shown that healers' brainwaves pulsate at a very low frequency, and after a while the patient's brainwaves will pulsate at the same frequency.

A very simple technique I use quite often is to adjust the aura. Sometimes I will see that a person's aura doesn't extend evenly all round the body as it should; it will bulge on one side and look very thin on the other. So I manipulate it until it's evenly balanced, lightening the areas that are too condensed. I also make sure that it comes down well below their feet; the aura extends downwards as well as all round and above the body.

An unbalanced aura can result from shock, stress or disease; the same thing can happen to the mind energy. Many times I've opened the door to someone and seen a bulge on one side of his head, like a hat worn on one side. When I ask, 'Do you find you're suffering from an imbalance?' he says: 'That's exactly what I've come to you about. I can't walk straight!'

This is because the bulging mind energy makes him feel one-sided, and afraid of falling over. People are sometimes diagnosed as having medical or neurological conditions, when all they have is unbalanced mind energy which can be put right very simply. Some people bump into things, or describe themselves as 'clumsy'. I've suffered from this myself: from childhood I was always banging into doors, or putting a cup down on a table only to have it crash to the floor.

Once I realized what was wrong, I cured myself overnight. It was shortly after the time when I looked in the mirror and realized that the eye I was seeing was one of my own. I saw my own mind energy in the mirror, too, and realized that it was protruding on one side. Feeling a bit silly, I put my hand up to my head and patted it as if it were untidy hair. To my surprise, I saw it moving into place. And after that my 'clumsiness' was gone! Since then, I have regularly treated myself by smoothing out my aura and mind energy.

Some people come to me after having every conceivable kind of hospital test, without a medical diagnosis being reached. In such cases clairvoyant diagnosis is a godsend. Many conditions which have baffled medical science are caused by negative energy pressing on a vital spot which undermines the efficient working of a major organ. Treatment applied to the organ alone does not remove the congestion which is at the root of the problem, and too often drugs actually cause more congestion within the body.

Take, for example, a man who came to me with high blood-pressure. Despite being treated by his doctor, and eventually by a consultant, his blood-pressure had steadily increased. When I viewed his energy system, I could see large areas of congested energy around the abdomen, in the groin and around the heart. Small areas of congestion were also scattered throughout the rest of his body.

I started by laying my hands on his abdomen, gradually easing the congestion and watching it as it cleared. When he came for his second appointment he told me his blood-pressure had already returned to a satisfactory level. He visited me four times in all, and when I last heard of him five years later his blood-pressure was still normal. He was just one of hundreds of people I have been able to relieve or cure in which high blood-pressure has been the main contributory factor, yet medical treatment has not touched the cause in the energy system.

An interesting illustration of the importance of the energy body is the case of 'phantom limbs', amputated limbs in which the unfortunate person still feels pain. Ask anyone who has had an arm amputated where their fingers are, and they will point to the area, and even hold the apparently empty air. They can feel the whole limb because its energy form is still present, and it is this excess energy, no longer attached to the physical, that causes the pain. Using a more powerful energy, the life force, can reduce the phantom limb to the same size as the remaining part of the physical limb. The pain factor can then either be greatly relieved or completely eliminated.

I have demonstrated clairvoyant diagnosis at seminars both in England and abroad. I ask for a subject from the audience and then go through his body from head to toe giving my findings; I also receive 'mind pictures' of past accidents and operations. Sometimes there have been doctors present who have backed up my diagnosis.

Anyone who treats the spine, like osteopaths and chiropractors, will understand the following story. I have taken part in several seminars at a well-known public school. At one of these I was working with a group including four of the masters, a doctor, and one or two other people. One of the masters told me he had been having terrible problems with his stomach for about six months; at one point he'd been dashed off to hospital in agony, but they hadn't been able to find out what was wrong.

I looked at him; I thought I could see what the trouble was but I wanted to be sure. I said: 'Would you mind very much lying face down on the floor?'

He obligingly lay down, wondering what I was up to. 'It's my *stomach*,' he said.

I said: 'Well, I want to see your spine.'

I told him I could see that he had a problem with one of his vertebrae, right between his shoulderblades.

'What's that got to do with my stomach?' he asked.

I said: 'To be honest, I don't know, but I know that when it's put right your stomach problems will go.'

At that point the doctor stepped in and said: 'My mother was an osteopath and taught me osteopathy. May I just go down the spine and have a look?'

He examined the man's spine, came to the same spot and said: 'You're absolutely right. Do you mind if I deal with it?' And there and then he manipulated the vertebra.

Afterwards he told me: 'You chose the only vertebra that can cause pressure on the part of the central nervous system that affects the stomach.' He was very surprised, because it was obvious that I have no medical background. 'I'll tell you something else,' he said. 'Unless you're an osteopath as well as a doctor, you wouldn't know about it.'

I've since been told that many of the mysterious pains that people experience in the chest and abdomen may be caused by problems in the spine. The schoolmaster had no further trouble with his stomach after this.

I am very careful about what I tell patients during diagnosis; I would never say anything that would frighten them or lead them to expect the worst. Sometimes you hear of healers making wild statements or alarming prognoses; I have been embarrassed to be present sometimes when so-called healers have given 'diagnoses' that were totally inaccurate. When this kind of thing happens, it's not surprising that doctors become wary about healers. It is vital to be responsible about what you see, and not to invent what you don't see! Any kind of diagnosis, medical or clairvoyant, is difficult. As a healer, I can only discuss it in terms of energy, negative or otherwise. The important thing is to get to the truth of what I am perceiving.

It would be interesting if some further research could be undertaken in which scientists could co-operate with psychics. We are still in the beginners' class as far as our knowledge of the mind is concerned!

Many more people would benefit if healing were used in conjunction with medical treatment. If there is to be a *complete* cure, the energy system must be sustained; problems recur because so often only the symptoms are treated, and not the cause. The ideal situation, which I would like to see much more often, is when doctors and healers can work hand in hand. One of my doctor patients who has become a healer himself has made the following comments:

> Unfortunately there is a lot of superstition associated with mediums, clairvoyants and healers. Betty has done a great deal of good for a very large number of people, including children with terminal illnesses. Many of the people who have been to see her, have found a great deal of peace and inner healing which seems to be lost from our society today. Whatever the British Medical Association would like to say about alternative medicine, healing does, in fact, work. The doctor is able to use his skills to cure a person, but seems to have lost the ability to 'heal'. In the same way that the cuts on our fingers are healed in the main without the intervention of medicine, our bodies are capable of tremendous healing given the necessary energy stimulus. Healers like Betty are in-valuable in that healing process.

TWO

The Experience of Healing

Healing should be a beautiful experience for both patient and healer. It's sad that people are still frightened of the 'unknown', when what they think of as the unknown is so peaceful and loving. When I am healing or giving counselling, a feeling of peace pervades the room. It is as though outside pressures no longer exist.

I have always kept my healing-rooms simple – no candles, no incense, no little red lamps! They are furnished with just a table or a desk, a couple of chairs and a medical couch on which the patient can sit back or lie in comfort. In Sutton I had the ceiling painted blue, which people found very peaceful to look at. In my present house, the room overlooks an enclosed part of the garden, which is also very peaceful.

A healing session lasts for half an hour to an hour, depending on the person's condition; I usually give an hour to people who are seriously ill. The healing itself doesn't take this long, but I need the time to talk with them and listen to their problems, and also to give them the clairvoyant advice and information which come through me while I heal.

I prefer it if people come having had a medical diagnosis and, if necessary, X-rays. Unfortunately, many people have had bad experiences with doctors and hospitals, and don't want any more to do with them. However, I would always encourage anyone who is having medical treatment to stay with it. (The very occasional exception is when I see that medical drugs are not only not helping but also actually damaging the system, as in Jenny's story on page 193.)

People often ask me if the patient has to have faith, to which I sometimes say: 'No, but *I* do!' I have healed some extremely sceptical people over the years. It is true that a receptive attitude and trust in the healer do help; without this kind of rapport the relationship is likely to be short-lived — the feeling is usually mutual, and visits cease of their own accord. Faith, however, is a different matter; it is very difficult to have faith in something until one has proof that it works. Incidentally, I think that calling healing 'faith healing' is very confusing, particularly as other labels such as 'spiritual healing' are used to describe the same phenomenon. As far as I'm concerned, everyone who heals from what I call 'the source' is simply a healer.

During healing nearly everyone becomes deeply relaxed; quite a few go to sleep on the healing-couch, and some feel exceptionally tired for at least twelve hours afterwards. This is because the energy counterpart of the physical body has been manipulated, vibrated and stimulated in an unaccustomed manner. When people are suffering from severe tension, simply being able to relax can bring about changes very rapidly. I also encourage them to help themselves by teaching relaxation techniques to practise at home.

The mother of one of my child patients came to see me with pains in her legs which, she said, 'felt like lead from morning to night'. Doctors had dismissed her complaint as 'a woman's problem'. By the time she came to see me she was, as she put it, 'totally lost, and wondering if I was losing my faculties'. I knew exactly how she felt, having been through plenty of stressful times myself. An ability to empathize is very reassuring to people under stress, particularly if they haven't been taken very seriously by their doctor.

As she lay on my couch with my hands on her, she told me she felt totally relaxed for the first time in what seemed like years; she could feel her legs tingling and the tension flowing out of her. She worked at practising relaxation and positive thinking at home, and has never been troubled with pains in her legs since that first visit.

One side-effect of relaxation is that everybody produces incredible tummy rumbles! Some people are rather embarrassed about these unspiritual sounds. 'I've just had lunch,' they'll say apologetically. 'It's not your lunch; it's the healing,' I explain. 'It's a good sign actually: it means the intestines are relaxing and releasing gases.' It even happens to people who aren't having healing themselves but are sitting in the same room.

I also deliberately use my ability to make people laugh if I think laughter will release the tension sufficiently to allow the healing energies to penetrate. It's fascinating to see what happens when someone laughs: the mind energy bursts through the top of the head as though from a steam engine – it looks as though people are literally 'letting off steam'.

Healing is very safe; in the thousands of years it has been used there has never been a recorded case of anyone being physically injured or dying as a result of it. It is just not possible – with healing, you simply can't give the wrong drug or perform the wrong operation! It is also very powerful. Many people underestimate its power because at the time all they experience is some tingling and heat, and a very calm period of relaxation. Then they phone me next day to tell me they have experienced phenomenal effects.

I have heard of people being disappointed in healing, especially if they have been misled by an over-optimistic healer, or of course by a charlatan – there are some around, unfortunately. It is a great pity when this happens. There are also some people who expect healers to be instant miracle-workers. It is true that instant miracles do occasionally happen, but for most people healing takes a little longer. If someone's energy is very depleted, several healings may be needed before their system is charged enough to affect the physical.

In some people the physical has deteriorated to such an

extent that no amount of energy can stimulate it to effect a cure. However, I never tell anyone at first meeting that I can't cure them, any more than I would guarantee a cure. I ask them about the medical prognosis – which is usually completely hopeless – and then try to find out where the problem is, what's happening, how the life force isn't getting through and why. To safeguard against disappointment on both sides, I usually suggest that they have four to six sessions, so that we can monitor the results. After this it should be clear whether they are reacting favourably or not. Even in seemingly impossible cases miraculous things have happened, and even those who are past curing can be relieved by the removal of congestion.

For the last two years I have been specializing in cases that have been labelled as hopeless, and I know that healing can not only remove pain but also extend lives well beyond the medical prognosis. Many terminally ill people have been able to enjoy their final months and have died peacefully, without pain, when according to all the medical forecasts they should have been in agony.

There are still people who insist that *all* healing must be psychosomatic. This is rubbish! For one thing, healing works just as well with animals as with humans – if not better, since they don't put up any barriers. (The vets who get the best results are those who, like some doctors, are natural healers.)

I had been healing animals without realizing it since I was a child. As a little girl, I made up for my mother's refusal to let me have a kitten by talking to every animal I met; there were plenty about in the streets, many of them strays. I found I had an empathy with them and, if they seemed unwell, just holding them in my arms made them better.

Animals love healing; they accept the energy and then usually go to sleep, often remaining flat out for the rest of the day! It would be wonderful if human beings could be so accepting and so relaxed, instead of rushing back to work or busy domestic duties! A period of rest and quiet is an essential part of the healing process.

I remember Mandy, a lovely golden retriever who had arthritic hips; the first time she arrived for healing, Mandy wagged her tail so hard she sent everything flying! It was as though she already knew that she would be cured. At each session she would settle herself down on the carpet; as soon as I placed my hands on her hips she would sigh with contentment, gazing trustingly up at me with her beautiful eyes. It was a joy when, a month later, after only four sessions, her arthritis was completely cured. Unfortunately, it isn't always possible to bring about a total cure with older animals, but healing can still help them to run instead of walk, and enjoy life to the full as long as they can.

Two years ago I had to give healing to Flossie, our miniature Yorkshire terrier. We have another bitch called Tessa, a black Labrador type; the two are very good friends, despite the fact that Tessa weighs forty pounds and Flossie only four! One day Alan was about to take them for a walk when Tessa, in her excitement, jumped up in the air and came down with all her weight on Flossie. Poor Flossie was completely flattened, and for some minutes Alan thought she was going to die.

For a few days we were quite concerned about her; however, we took her to the vet and I gave her masses of healing, and she was up and about a week after her mishap. But some time later we discovered a lump in her groin, which was obviously causing her discomfort. Alan immediately took her back to the vet, who diagnosed a large hernia which had to be operated on. We were very worried at the idea of her having an anaesthetic as she is so tiny, so I gave her intense healing over the five days before the operation was due.

When the day arrived Alan took her to the vet; instead of leaving her with his assistant, he asked for the vet to examine her first. After a thorough investigation the vet exclaimed: 'But the hernia's gone!'

Alan told him that I was a healer and had been giving Flossie healing, but the vet simply repeated; 'Yes, but it's disappeared!' He couldn't understand it at all! He said: 'You'd better take her home. There's nothing for me to do, but please contact me immediately if it recurs.' I am delighted to say that it hasn't.

Humans, of course, are suggestible, and the mind undoubtedly plays a very important part in both health and sickness. But during healing I see clear changes in the body's energy system which cannot be due to suggestion. There are often very marked physical effects, too; indeed, the energy factor can sometimes be quite unnerving.

Early on in my work I was healing a man who was crippled with arthritic knees. He was a Beefeater, and extremely upset as he'd set his heart on gaining the Queen's Long Service Medal. He had only eighteen months to go, but now the state of his knees prevented him from standing for long periods – in fact he could hardly walk, and then only with a stick.

As I was healing him there was a sudden loud crack, just as though someone had fired a gun. I nearly fell off my stool! Then I realized that the calcium in his knee-joints had somehow exploded. When he stood up he was already able to walk much better. After three months' weekly treatments he was able to resume his job and he did receive his medal. He deserved it!

These cracks and explosions were repeated again and again with arthritic cases, and they always came as a surprise both to me and to the person I was healing. Another very physical phenomenon has occurred in cases of kidney- and gall-stones, when calcium stones have actually appeared on the surface of the abdomen while I have been healing! With osteoarthritis the unwanted bone seems simply to dematerialize. I have asked people to try to obtain 'before' and 'after' X-rays, so that they can see the changes that have taken place; unfortunately, hospitals are too busy to take extra X-rays merely out of interest!

One 'side-effect' which sometimes alarms people is the appearance of bruising the following day. This happens most often when I have been giving treatment for an internal infection or some kind of muscular pain; it's as if, on its way out, the condition surfaces in the form of a bruise, sometimes very colourfully.

Just recently I gave healing to Jean, a friend who was helping to type this book. She had a thrombosis seventeen years ago, and had very bad varicose veins. Healing is very effective with varicose veins; I can actually feel them slipping underneath my hands as they straighten out, and they did on this occasion.

Afterwards Jean took her usual walk home, across a field. When she came to climb the stile she felt as though somebody actually lifted her up and over – 'I was so light I couldn't feel myself on the ground,' she told me. But she rang me up in alarm next morning because her legs were so bruised; she thought something must have gone terribly wrong! I assured her it was quite normal, and actually a good sign. As always, the bruising disappeared after twelve hours, and her veins are now in excellent condition.

Jean also experienced another extraordinary side-effect which you are unlikely to find in any medical textbook. I had been giving her absent healing for a back condition when she rang me up in great excitement to tell me about 'the most incredible experience she'd ever had in her life'. While she was having her bath that morning the water had turned bright blue!

This phenomenon has happened only three times in my experience; once, when I was living in Sutton, it happened to me. I had been overworking and was so tired that I fell asleep in the bath; when I woke up the water was a bright electric blue. I couldn't think what had happened, and kept looking round to see whether something had fallen into the bath, although I knew nothing could have done.

I lay there thinking: I don't believe this! I never get over the wonder of this kind of experience. Although I use colour a lot in healing, I have no idea where this blue came from.

I use a number of specific techniques in addition to laying on of hands. One, which I call the 'laser beam', is for conditions such as cellular congestion, meridian lines that are hard to unblock, or any area which is not responding to ordinary healing. I use it especially for eye problems. With my mind I form a 'laser beam' of powerful energy, like a very fine steel rod, and direct it towards the trouble-spot until it clears.

I use my mind to do other things, too, such as 'operating' to remove congested energy. For example, if there is an energy congestion in the stomach caused by stress, I create mental instruments and make a cut down the body, so that I can pull out the tangle of energy just like a ball of wool. Sometimes it goes on for a long time, until suddenly the last bit is pulled free. Then I use the 'laser beam' to seal up the cut.

You may say: 'But that's just imagination.' That is to underestimate the power of the imagination. Once you realize its possibilities, whatever you want to do with your mind you can do: the thought is the deed. I don't tell people what I am doing until afterwards, but while it's going on they say: 'My God, that feels better! I feel as if something's been released!'

While I am healing I also receive a lot of clairvoyant information to pass on to my patients, sometimes from dead relatives, sometimes from other spirit helpers. When people first get in touch with me I always tell them I'm a medium. Some of them don't want to know about this side of my work; I respect this, and if one of their dead relatives tries to come through I will convey to them telepathically that the healing is more important. But everything I have learned I have been taught, directly or indirectly, by spirit minds; sometimes the phenomena that occur during healing can only be accounted for by their activities, and they can't be ignored! Sometimes they take over altogether.

At the start of a session I usually chat for a while to put people at their ease. But there usually comes a moment when I say: 'I won't be speaking to you for a little while. And maybe I will take my hands away from you.'

When I sense that other minds want to come in and work with mine, I must allow them that space. I will suddenly feel a tremendous power coming in, like a physical force, always on my left-hand side. Then I know that somebody else's mind has connected with mine, and I start receiving clairvoyant diagnosis which is more detailed than my initial assessment. If I feel it will be helpful I pass this information on to the person concerned.

My healing gifts have been developed by invisible teachers – invisible to other people, that is, because at times they are quite visible to me. I may just glimpse them, but sometimes I see them with tremendous vividness. I know intuitively that they are doctors and scientists; quite often I see them standing round the patient, just like hospital consultants, looking at each other and working together. They don't speak, but I am aware that they are very powerful beings.

I've been asked why someone who died perhaps fifty years ago should be up to date with treatments. The question made me laugh, because they are probably wondering why *we* are so backward! However, the answer is that doctors and scientists in the next dimension are not working with matter. Those who choose to receive a further education, as it were, are trained to work with the energy fields, which is quite different from working with the physical.

Some healers work with a single guide, and I've occasionally been asked whether I've 'got' a Red Indian or a Chinaman. I haven't. There are many minds involved in the healing of many different diseases. If I'm working with a disease like cancer, I don't want to be limited to a single source of help. After all, some doctor with a brilliant mind may die tomorrow; he may then be able to come in and help me, and I wouldn't want to shut him out!

I've always felt very privileged with the minds that come through. When I start healing I just close my eyes and say mentally: Give me the best you've got. On one occasion, faced with a woman in appalling pain from a phantom limb, I simply thought: Surely somebody out there must be able to help this poor devil! Instantly she said: 'I don't believe it – my arm feels like a heavy block, but the pain has gone!' My request may not have been very reverent, but I think it was its fervency that instantaneously drew the right kind of help.

When a superior mind connects with mine, I feel totally elated. Sometimes the power is so strong that I know I must put my own hands aside and let them take over. I warn the patient what's happening, but even then they can be very surprised. Recently I was healing a bank manager; I was sitting at his head when he said: 'Someone's holding my feet, Betty!'

'I did tell you I'm a medium.'

'Yes, yes, but someone's holding my feet!'

To people who haven't experienced this kind of thing, it sounds a bit frightening, I know. When it actually happens to you, it isn't. This man was fascinated by the experience, and some people find it quite beautiful and moving. Sometimes people feel their faces being gently stroked. One couple who came to see me felt hands being gently laid on their chests as they lay in bed that night. They both became so beautifully relaxed that they went straight to sleep; only at breakfast next morning did they discover that they had both felt the same thing at exactly the same time.

You could go into all sorts of hypothetical explanations for their experience. Were they both imagining it? Did their minds link telepathically? In the end I can only describe what people have felt and seen, and what I have felt and seen myself. This couple knew nothing about healing beforehand; these are the kind of people I listen to, because their experience is genuine and unadulterated by preconceived ideas.

I know that I am just a channel for all these wonderful things, and I think it's terribly sad that only a small proportion of people are convinced that they can really happen. It's lovely when a patient who doesn't really believe suddenly opens his eyes and says: 'Goodness, are you over there? But I thought you were holding my feet. Somebody is!'

Even more dramatic is when a psychic manipulation or operation is performed, while I stand back and watch it happen. Manipulation is something that has built up slowly in my experience. One of the earliest occasions was with a man called Fred; he and his wife Shirley are long-standing friends of mine and have come in for several interesting experiences. Fred seldom enjoys them.

On this occasion I was giving him healing when his arm suddenly started moving. 'My arm's going up and down!' he said in alarm. 'Betty, why's my arm going up and down?' I tried to calm him by explaining that he was being manipulated by unseen helpers. His eyes widened even more and he said, 'I don't think I like this.' (Since those days, Shirley herself has become very psychic, and Fred has learned to live with it!)

The most powerful manipulation I ever witnessed was about ten years ago. David was a young amateur footballer who visited me a lot because he was always damaging himself. He arrived one day in a state of desperation: he had smashed his foot and ankle very badly, and the hospital had told him they could do nothing more for him. He was accompanied by his father, who watched the whole session.

Whilst I was healing David, a voice asked me to take my hands away. I told him what I was going to do and why, and moved well away from him. Then we all three watched in amazement as the injured leg was lifted up, pushed about and thoroughly manipulated. I have said that healing is painless, and most of the time it is, but in this instance I could tell from his voice and expression that David was in considerable pain.

After it was over, however, he was able to get down from the couch and walk about absolutely normally and painlessly. His father said: 'Betty, if I hadn't seen this for myself I would never have believed it!'

While they were still there the unseen manipulator informed me that he had been a physiotherapist and trainer with a famous football team. He had died in an air-crash which was widely reported at the time, and now wanted to heal athletes through me. He went into some detail about the crash, giving me the names of the people who had survived, which enabled me to check and confirm his identity. He was a very well-known trainer in his lifetime, and obviously a very compassionate man whose compassion continued after his death.

Sometimes I am told to stand aside to allow a psychic operation to be performed. The first time it happened was with a lady in her seventies suffering from diverticulitis. I told her that I was going to take my hands away, and a moment later she said: 'Betty, I can feel hands inside me, doing something right down inside of me! I really can feel hands!' Again, this sounds much weirder than it actually is. People find it unusual, certainly, but not at all unpleasant or painful.

It is fascinating to watch: I can see hands moving over and inside the patient's body; sometimes I see the faces of the spirit surgeons, too. These operations are nothing like the psychic surgery practised in the Philippines, which is reportedly accompanied by lots of blood and mess. The people for whom I am a channel operate on the energy counterpart only.

One young woman was due to have a hysterectomy for fibroids when she was recommended to see me. A psychic operation was decided on, and as I watched I could see the energy counterparts of the fibroids, three opaque lumps of energy, actually being lifted out of her body and then disappearing. She could feel hands inside her, but no pain at all. When she went back to the hospital they could find nothing to operate on! It seems that by removing the congestion in the energy counterpart the operation enabled the physical fibroids to shrink and vanish from the body.

The energy counterparts of our organs are not duplications of the physical organs, in the sense of having all the cells and blood-vessels and so on; it is simply that the energy occupying that area of the body takes on the shape of the organ concerned. When there is a problem with, say, the womb, the liver or a kidney, that part of the body has become congested with negative energy which must be released. The spirit doctors work on it by removing the energy form, reviving and re-energizing it, and perhaps rebalancing energies which have become distorted in some way. When they return the revitalized energy form to the body it stimulates the physical organ into action. Sometimes I do this operation myself, drawing the energy out with my hands and stimulating it before stroking it back in.

I am always aware of guidance and have learned to trust my impressions totally. For instance, when I started using colour healing I thought for a time that I had to work out what colours were needed and how to project them. Then I realized that the appropriate colours were being beamed down anyway. I don't know whether it is the healer's energy or the patient's need that attracts colours, but they arrive unasked for, and it is clear that there are spirit helpers who know which ones to give.

Nearly all my clients see colours to some degree while being healed. Sometimes two or three shades come in together like a rainbow, and play around the patient. One beautiful example of this was when I was healing a young woman who was herself very psychic. She was lying there with her eyes open, when she said: 'Betty, can you see what I see?'

I said: 'Tell me what you can see.'

Then she described a whole spectrum of colours –

greens, blues, yellows and purple – which I, too, was seeing. 'Isn't that wonderful!' she exclaimed. It was. It looked exactly as if they were being beamed down by someone with a spotlight.

I have had so many experiences like these that I can be in no doubt that other minds work through mine, in a mind-to-mind contact. It seems that my part is to provide an energy field which allows the spirit healers to come in and do their work. They are obviously people who have used these skills before, and want to continue using them for the good of mankind. The energy that comes from them is extremely powerful; the patient can often feel it, and may describe it as 'electricity on their face' or 'feeling electrified'. As a result, the whole healing-room becomes charged with energy. For a long time now it's been almost impossible for me to tape-record anything in this room without tremendous interference.

These days I usually put a new tape on to record while I'm healing; I ask people to bring their own. My healing-room is very quiet, and when they hear the rec-orded sound people find it very reassuring to have positive proof that there are extraordinary energies in action.

Another therapy I use quite often came to me as a total surprise. When I had been healing for five or six years I went to see Nella Taylor, a very talented medium. She knew absolutely nothing about me beforehand, but she told me: 'You used your voice for singing; over and over again you went up the ladder and you were pushed down again. That's because your voice wasn't meant to be used in that medium; it was meant to be used in the medium in which you are now working.'

Now she tells me! I thought. But I couldn't make out what she meant, unless she was referring to the fact that people felt better when they heard my voice over the telephone.

About a year later, I was healing a boy of thirteeen who had a bed-wetting problem. He was nicely relaxed and we were chatting about his school work when I felt a powerful presence coming in. Then I heard myself speaking in a quiet voice. 'Close your eyes,' I told him, with no idea why I was saying it. 'You will feel your eyelids become heavy. You will not be able to open your eyes; you will not want to open your eyes. Your body is becoming heavier and heavier. You will never wet the bed again.' I repeated this several times.

The child was by now in a meditative state, though his occasional remarks showed that he was aware of everything that was going on. The whole session lasted about twenty minutes. Still allowing myself to be guided, I brought him back to normal alertness.

He had thoroughly enjoyed the experience. 'Gosh,' he said, 'that was marvellous! I felt as if I was flying, and I saw all these marvellous colours.' He never wet the bed again.

Like so many things that have happened to me, this experience was totally unexpected. Somebody – I had no idea who – had definitely taken over and guided me.

Some time later I was passing a secondhand bookshop with Leslie when I told him: 'I've got to go in. There's a book in there I have to have!' Inside, I went straight to a thick, closely printed volume on hypnosis by a Dr Albert Moll, first published in 1889. (I have never seen his name mentioned anywhere else.) When I got home I sat down and read it, and as I did so I had the odd experience of knowing exactly what was going to come next.

I had never had it in mind to apply hypnosis to anyone, and it was something I avoided having done to me. Like many people, I didn't like the idea of someone else's mind taking over mine. However, ever since then I have used hypnotherapy regularly in conjunction with healing, when it's appropriate. It has proved invaluable with allergic conditions, which are often stress-related, and I also use it to help people give up smoking or to slim. I explain to the person concerned that I am not taking over their mind, and ask them to tell me what they would like me to suggest to them so that we are both working together. Usually they want to be turned off sugar or cigarettes or something similar, and using hypnosis I am therefore working on their suggestions and not mine.

An important aspect of my work is absent or distant healing: giving healing to someone who may be hundreds of miles away. It is a wonderful example of the power of mind energy, which has no limitations and can travel any distance. I have given absent healing to people all over the world, and have acquired total faith in it. The success rate is phenomenal, and I recommend it as an alternative to contact healing, particularly if people live far away or are too ill to travel – including accident victims in coma. When the first contact is made I ask the person concerned, or somebody close to them, to phone me weekly to keep me up to date with their progress. In nine out of ten cases I receive a phone call within twenty-four hours informing me that the sick person is already much better.

I am usually contacted by phone, and also quite often by letter, with the patient's name and a description of the medical problem. As soon as I'm given the name I get a clairvoyant diagnosis. This can be very useful, as in the case of a woman who rang me from America to ask for help as she had been feeling unwell for some time without being able to discover the cause. As we were speaking I learned clairvoyantly that she had diabetes. On my advice she went to see a specialist who confirmed the diagnosis. I gave her absent healing every day for two or three weeks, and at her next appointment with the specialist he told her that the condition had completely cleared.

In absent as in contact healing I know that it isn't all up to me, and the first thing I do is to ask whoever's listening: 'Will you please help this person?' If you have an expansive mind – a mind that extends out to other minds and other dimensions – someone will be listening, and they will always respond. I understand from communication with the minds of the so-called 'dead' that a medium's mind shines like a beacon in other dimensions.

I know this to be true and that my thoughts are being picked up and acted upon. The power of thought is a power to be reckoned with!

In giving absent healing, my own part is to visualize the person, if I know them, or the affected part of the body if I don't; I then project energy specifically to where it's needed. As with contact healing, I don't limit myself to one specific technique. For instance, I use my 'laser beam' on people who have lost their sight, and on other problems where it's appropriate; I find it remarkably effective.

Here's a typical example of how absent healing works. Louise, a close friend of mine, was on a motoring holiday with her husband in France. She had misguidedly driven from Burgundy to Geneva and back, over mountain roads, in one day; the next day her back hurt so much she could hardly move. Her husband couldn't drive, and they had to get back to Calais; so, feeling quite desperate, she rang me up and asked for help.

I told her: 'Go back to your room, sit quietly, and ring me back in twenty minutes.'

I immediately asked for help; then, using visualization, I projected energy towards her from the top to the bottom of her back. Louise told me afterwards that when she went to her room she sat down with a book but – just at the time when I was manipulating energy up and down her spine – an extraordinarily powerful feeling of warmth stole over her. She put her book down and simply sat still and soaked it in. After twenty minutes she got up easily, almost without a twinge, and rang to thank me. She drove home feeling better than she had for the whole of the holiday.

Time, space, scepticism and even total unawareness on behalf of the recipient do not detract in any way from this form of energy manipulation. A woman once asked me to give absent healing to her brother-in-law in Australia who was about to have an operation for cancer, with only a fifty-fifty chance of recovery. After working out the time difference, I sat down quietly and sent out healing energies while the operation was taking place.

Some time later, during a post-operative examination, the surgeon remarked that he had experienced an extraordinary phenomenon whilst operating. He said: 'The heat coming from your body was unbelievable. I have never known anything like it. Can you account for it?'

The patient was as bewildered as the surgeon. Unfortunately his wife, feeling he would be sceptical, told him nothing, and he has no idea to this day that he was receiving healing, or the reason for the heat. But when I last heard of him he was doing well.

I quite often tune in to the patient's surroundings. Giving absent healing at a friend's request to her little niece in a New York hospital, I became aware that there was a huge toy bear standing by the bed. I was puzzled by the size of it; it was the sort of thing you see at fairs or in window displays, but not usually in hospitals. When my friend called next day I mentioned it to her, and she promised to make enquiries. Three days later she phoned to say the child's mother had bought an outsize toy bear and stood it by her daughter's bed on the day when I had given healing.

This ability to observe from a distance can be extremely useful, especially if someone is very sick. I may learn, for example, that the circumstances they are living in are making them worse, and can then suggest ways to improve them.

Absent healing can also work in reverse. A sick person who thinks about me can automatically contact the healing energies around me and receive help, even if I'm not aware of it myself. One day Alan was in terrible pain with back trouble; he was without his car and about to walk up a very steep hill. He stood still and thought of me, saying: 'Betty, please help me.' The effect was immediate, the pain went, and he climbed the hill effortlessly. Everyone who visits me for healing has tried thinking of me in this way at some time or other, and no one has been disappointed.

Just recently I had a letter from an elderly patient with cancer; he was lying in bed quite ill, he wrote, when 'a lady appeared'. Although she didn't look like me, she reminded him of me. At that point his wife came into the room to tell him that I had just phoned and had been giving him absent healing. Other people have recognized me by their bed when they have been ill. I believe this experience is quite common among healers.

As with contact healing, absent healing can produce some quite powerful effects. I've told you about Fred, who was scared when his arm was manipulated. A couple of years later his wife Shirley phoned to say he was in hospital after having a heart-attack, and please would I help. She gave me the name of the hospital, and I told her that healing would begin immediately.

That evening, after visiting the hospital, she phoned me again. Fred had asked her if I was giving him healing; when she told him I was, he said: 'Would you please tell her to stop, because I levitated off my bed and I was frightened to death!'

This feeling of levitation is very common. People don't actually levitate physically but, because the energy counterpart is being stimulated and there is so much energy around, it *feels* as if the body is weightless and floating. Despite Fred's alarm, the healing was very effective: he underwent numerous tests, but no trace was found of the after-effects of a heart-attack or of any other form of illness.

Another very physical phenomenon occurred with a man who didn't believe in absent healing. He came with his wife, and while I was healing her he asked if I could do anything for his ingrowing toe-nail: he had suffered pain in his toe for years and had been to doctors and chiropodists to no avail. When I said I would give him absent healing he thought I was joking and laughed. I pointed my finger at him and said: 'Wait and see!'

88

When they returned a week later he told me that two days after that last visit he had been in agony. To relieve the pain he had lifted his toe-nail away from the flesh with a nail-file – whereupon, a calcium ball the size of a small pea had popped out.

It was obvious that this had been *inside* the toe, pressing the flesh up against the nail and causing pain all these years, not an ingrowing toe-nail at all; this kind of calcium formation can occur with some arthritic conditions, like gout. He and his wife examined the toe with a magnifying glass but could find no sign of the place where it had come through the skin, not so much as a pin-hole. After that, he had no further trouble with his toe.

Although this type of phenomenon had occurred before whilst giving healing it was the first time it had happened with absent healing. I was sorry to learn that they'd thrown the calcium ball away. I'd have liked to see it.

Absent healing is wonderful for animals, and I've treated more animals in this way than by contact healing. It can deal with a surprising range of problems. One summer, a friend asked me if I could do something for her dog who had insect bites all over his body. She had applied a variety of lotions to no avail, and the vet had told her that many other dogs in the neighbourhood had the same problem. It was a beautiful summer, and the grass everywhere was infested, so that every time the dog was taken for a run it was bitten all over!

What I did was to visualize a protective coat of energy all around the dog. Two days later my friend told me there was no sign of any further bites. This happy situation lasted throughout the summer even though other animals continued to get infested!

About ten years ago, I discovered that it is possible not only to protect an animal against insects, but also to communicate with the insects themselves. Janet and I were sitting in the garden in Sutton on a beautifully still and sunny day when we suddenly found ourselves covered with flying ants. For the next hour they wouldn't leave us alone; we were very annoyed, because we had been enjoying a rare break to sunbathe. Eventually, Janet had had enough, and ran indoors for cover. I called out after her that I would speak to them – really intending it as a joke. However, I thought: Why not? Although they are a different species, we share the same life force and the same planet with them.

I sat quietly in the sun, covered in ants, and closed my eyes. I asked them to leave us alone, and directed them to an overgrown patch at the end of the garden. Almost immediately they began to leave. Soon the garden, which had been covered with little winged bodies, was totally ant-free. I called Janet, who found it hard to believe that I had done it – even I thought it could be a fluke. So after that I experimented for a while, to see whether it was or not.

Not long after the flying ants episode a South African visited me for healing for back trouble; as we talked he asked me jokingly if I could 'do anything' with animals – his home in South Africa was overrun by wild dogs. I thought it would be fun to have a go, and asked me next time he came to bring me a large-scale map of the area. He brought the map, and after his next healing session we studied it together. I asked him to show me an area where I could direct the dogs to go, where they wouldn't be such a nuisance. He picked a spot, and I told him I would do my best.

With his back better and his holiday over, the South African returned home. I worked telepathically on the dogs, asking them to leave his home and go to the designated area; after a month, as I hadn't heard from him, I stopped. Then, four months after he had left, the South African telephoned me out of the blue. He told me that the wild dogs had left his property three months before – but the biggest surprise of all was when he had passed the place we'd chosen to send them to. He had never seen so many dogs in one area, looking – by wild dog standards

– fit and well. They had obviously found a good food-supply.

Over the next few years I persuaded cockroaches, moles, wasps, bees and other unwanted creatures to move to other quarters! Mediumship is rather like owning a rough diamond that has to have every facet polished before it becomes whole and powerful. This particular gift was the polishing of another facet. After a time, I realized that I was quite often performing these feats simply as demonstrations and that I was dissipating valuable energy that I should be using for healing. So I will only do this now if it is genuinely affecting someone's physical or mental health.

However, I still believe that before deciding to finish off so-called pests – who have a perfect right to be here – it's worthwhile trying to contact them to ask for their co-operation. Why not try it yourself? One important point is that they should always be directed towards a *safe* place. There must never be any intention to eliminate them, which would be completely contrary to the purpose of healing energies and mind energy.

One day I had a frantic call from a friend of a friend whose daughter's bedroom had been invaded by ants; they were creeping in and out of the cracks in the plaster, and the little girl was so terrified she had to be moved out of her room. I asked for the address, and also for the location of a place where the ants could safely go as an alternative dwelling. After some discussion, we agreed on a large pile of old leaves and branches which would not be used for a bonfire.

Using the same method as with the dogs, I sat down and mentally communicated with the ants, explaining that they would be killed if they stayed, but would be quite safe if they moved down the garden to the woodpile. I did this twice a day for two days.

On the third day the woman phoned to tell me that the ants had suddenly gathered together and marched out of the window like an army! Her husband had followed them, and they actually finished up in the woodpile we had directed them to. The couple had plastered over the cracks in the walls, and their little girl was happily back in her own bed. They found it quite unbelievable.

For large animals like horses absent healing is a wonderful answer, particularly when they are suffering from emotional problems. Animals are just as capable of suffering from stress and loss of self-esteem as human beings, as I learned in particular from a horse.

I was contacted one day by a man who told me that a stable-girl at the riding school he attended was very concerned about one of the horses in her care. The horse had a large bald patch on his side which was permanently raw, and whenever he went out he started to limp and had to be returned to his stable. He had been taken to an equestrian hospital off and on for two years, but they could do nothing for him.

I asked for the horse's name and the location of the stables. With this information in my mind I sat down, closed my eyes and found myself immediately in telepathic contact with the horse. I learned that he was very unhappy: he had once been a racehorse and had loved the roar of the crowds. However, following a leg injury he was sold for private use, which he hated. He disliked the stables, and he was distressed at having been given a new name.

I was given his real name, and telepathically I promised him that it would be returned to him. I also suggested that he should think of himself as 'King of the Stables', which he surely was.

Five days later, I had a phone call from the stable-girl to say that the patch on the horse's side had healed and he no longer limped. She also told me that her employer had been furious when she found out that she had consulted a healer, and had nearly sacked the poor girl. However, she confirmed that I had been given the horse's correct original name, and she informed the owner that he must restore this to keep his horse happy. The owner and myself never communicated directly, but he must have taken notice because I heard that the horse continued to be healthy and apparently happy.

Six months later the man who had first told me of the horse's plight came to see me, absolutely delighted. After his usual weekly ride he had visited the horse's stable, and there above the door was painted his original name, just as I had promised. Who knows how my unseen friends had managed to influence the owner?

Just recently I had another occasion to have telepathic communication with a horse; this one belonged to Alan's secretary, Caroline. She was delighted when she first acquired Talisman, and he was a popular topic of conversation in the office. After a few weeks, however, Alan noticed that Caroline wasn't herself and asked her rather tentatively whether she had a problem. She told him she was upset because she would probably have to sell her horse; he had become exceedingly difficult to catch, and she often had to give up after chasing him round the field for hours. She was worn out!

That evening, when Alan told me about Caroline's problem, I said I would have a word with Talisman. Straight away I sat down, closed my eyes, and visualized Caroline with her horse. Using his name, I was able to make telepathic contact with him; probably a few horse-loving minds also linked up with me to help. I conveyed to him that life would be more peaceful if he obeyed Caroline's call.

Next day, when Alan asked after her horse, Caroline said: 'I can't believe it! Last night he came straight to the gate when I called him!' Talisman has behaved perfectly ever since.

There is one snag. Every time Caroline calls Talisman, the two horses with whom he shares a field also come galloping up and try to follow him through the gate! Alan has told me I must be more selective in future!

Although holding a telepathic conversation with a horse may sound a little odd to some people, I don't think any real animal-lover will find it that unusual; Barbara

Woodhouse, for instance, seems to have had a very similar gift. After all, people have had telepathic relationships with their animals since the beginning of time.

For mind-to-mind communication to take place in this way, animals must have a certain amount of mind energy. I have never studied it as I have in humans, but when I look at animals I can see a glow around them. Some animals are quite psychic and attuned, and it must be their mind energy that enables lost cats and dogs to travel long distances and find their way home.

Because of the incredible power of thought, absent healing can be carried out quite rapidly. If I have an enormous number of people to heal, I simply put all their letters together, or write their names on a sheet of paper; I put my hands on them, close my eyes and put energy into them, saying mentally: Please help everyone here. That's all that's needed: the thought is the deed.

I find it surprising that some people are sceptical about the power of absent healing, yet still expect to get results from prayer. They pray to someone or something they can't see or even begin to comprehend and yet they have such faith. I very rarely pray for help, because I feel strongly that having been given a mind I should use it in a positive manner all the time instead of asking someone else to do the job for me. When I give absent healing I *know* there are minds picking up information and organizing the energies, but I also visualize and use my own mind in a positive way.

I believe more prayers would be answered if the people asking for help also did something positive at the same time. Somewhere along the line we must become self-responsible. Each one of us has been given mind energy to use. We should allow it to strengthen and expand, not keep it imprisoned within the confinement of limited beliefs.

All the same, there have been occasions when absent healing has been taken completely out of my hands; it's as if, the moment I'm told about a problem, someone has already seen to it. When I first met my agent, John, he told me he had suffered from a severe wheat allergy for five years. He had to be extremely careful what he ate, and his wife baked special bread for him. I said: 'Oh, I'll do something about that for you!'

Afterwards, though, I was so busy thinking about our discussion that I completely forgot! Two days later I was sitting in the sun-lounge day-dreaming when a voice said: 'Ring John and tell him he's been cured.'

I felt very guilty as I'd forgotten all about it. I rang John at once and passed on the message. Although he'd previously been sceptical, something must have convinced him, because he said: 'Right! I'll have a wheat day tomorrow.'

Still feeling guilty, I thought I'd better back up the cure with some absent healing. But as soon as I started to direct energy towards him I was blocked. I tried again, and was blocked again. Then a voice said: 'The job has been done; the job is finished.'

It was comforting to know that as soon as John had told me his problem the message had been received and dealt with.

No matter where you are in the world, absent healing can bring peace and a cure. It is also extraordinary how people have been mentally uplifted by the influence of the healing energies, with absent healing just as much as with contact healing. Their friends remark on how they have changed and how much more positive their outlook has become.

I have given absent healing to more people than I can possibly remember, but there are a few that stay with me, especially children, and I shall be writing about some of these later on. I have many times been asked to help children who have been given only a short time to live; after absent healing they have recovered rapidly. Although I am used to the powerful effects of healing, such cases still make me believe in miracles.

THREE

Mediumship

The public at large love to look upon mediums as mysterious, magical or evil, depending on what stimulates them most! I would like to explain some of the mysteries surrounding mediumship and try to correct the distorted image that many people conjure up in their minds when the word is mentioned.

Most people are unaware of the energies that surround us all, and even those who are aware may not give much thought to them. Why should they? Earning a living and looking after a family are enough to occupy most people's minds. It is only when things go wrong and the normal channels prove inadequate to help that people look for someone who can offer them hope and peace.

Perhaps you have lost a partner or a relative. You may have heard about survival evidence, but you are frightened to visit a medium because you have heard peculiar stories about them. Let me reassure you. When you visit a reputable medium you will probably come face to face with a quite ordinary-looking person, who will certainly put you at your ease. If you find yourself with any other kind – don't go back!

Practically all professional mediums and healers are down-to-earth ordinary people who do not consider themselves to be special. They use their talents every day and accept them as normal rather than as paranormal. Just as with any gift – whether it's music, carpentry or surgery – the more the gift is used, the more adept the user becomes.

To be a medium is to be a teacher: mediums are fed with information for the benefit of mankind. We none of us know it all, but at least we can use our professional skills to help others to learn. All types of teacher are needed today; not least, truly spiritual teachers – who should not be confused with religious teachers, not all of whom could be described as spiritual!

I have only visited four mediums in my life, all of whom were excellent. If I need help for anything, from medicine to car maintenance, I always try to find the most talented and highly recommended professional. Seeking a medium should be exactly the same; if you don't want to be disappointed or misled, be sure to choose the very best. Recommendation from someone who has already been helped is usually the safest way, but if you don't know of anyone personally there are organizations you can contact. (Two are listed at the end of the book.)

My healing work and my mediumship constantly overlap. Healing, I must confess, is my first love and a tremendous challenge. However, clairvoyance and survival evidence have a very important place in my work, showing as they do the extraordinary powers of mind energy, and proving that the mind survives the death of the physical body.

'Survival evidence' is the term used to describe messages from people who are 'dead'. Mediums receive them either in the form of telepathic communication from a dead person or by actually 'hearing' their voice, through clairaudience. There are many different ways of hearing: voices may be heard inside or outside your head, or the thought may just appear telepathically in your mind. More often than not the medium simultaneously receives a clairvoyant picture, which enables him to describe the speaker to the sitter.

Clairvoyance means 'clear seeing'; it is the gift of clear vision, usually into the future, and it has been used to help people throughout the ages. It is an extension of the faculty of intuition, which everyone has to some extent, and differs from survival evidence in that it does not necessarily involve direct communication from individual minds. My own explanation is that I tune in to universal energies, rather like turning on a television set, and receive words and pictures as though I am plugging into a vast telecommunications system.

There are several ways of receiving clairvoyance. Some seven years ago I was given a lot of information about my own future and my family's through automatic writing. I found myself covering sheets of paper every day; a great deal of it has already come true, and I know there is more to come!

Clairvoyance also enables you to see into the past. A few years ago I visited Biggin Hill with some friends. I was sitting quietly in the sun while they looked at the planes when suddenly the scene changed dramatically. I was taken back to the time of the Second World War; I watched, fascinated, as men in wartime flying gear and fitters in dungarees rushed to and fro. This flashback must have been only a few minutes long, but it seemed to last for ever.

I find that most of the clairvoyance I receive is positive. I never forecast disasters; indeed, I am rarely given negative information, though I may get warnings which can avert unhappiness if they are heeded. There are some mediums who predict disasters and death; this is thoroughly irresponsible. Even if I received such information I would question whether I was a hundred per cent right. But, being a very positive person myself, I only attract positive minds.

I do have some reservations about clairvoyance, however. For some people, wanting to know the future can become a sort of drug: they want it again and again, especially when they are given information that turns out to be accurate. Like any form of addiction this can be dangerous, negating the person's independence and self-responsibility.

I have also been told many times by clients that after having received clairvoyance they feel that they can sit back and allow things to happen. Then, when the predicted events don't happen straight away, they become frustrated and sometimes angry. When I realized that people were sitting back and doing nothing I felt quite upset, and didn't want to give any more clairvoyance – in fact my friends think I'm mean because I am unwilling to give them sittings. But I honestly find that, much more effective than predicting wonderful futures, is to tell people about mind energy and encourage them to use it to create their own wonderful futures!

Three years before I met Alan I visited a medium in London who told me that the man with whom I was to share the rest of my life would come to live with me when the daffodils were out. Every year as the daffodils came and went, I used to joke about it. 'Where is this man?' I'd complain to Janet. But I didn't take it too seriously, and carried on with the rest of my life.

I love daffodils, and one autumn I planted a thousand bulbs in my garden. It was about a month later that Michael Bentine told me that the man who would share my life would be with me in the spring. The following March, Alan and I were enjoying together the most beautiful spring I can ever remember, with daffodils everywhere we went! I should also have been told to plant my own!

Simply waiting for things to happen is negative. I teach positivity and self-help; negativity of any kind is harmful, not only to ourselves but also to those around us. However, giving clairvoyance is a part of my work, and it is always interesting when my predictions are fulfilled. This can take time: clairvoyance may show you the end of the road, but not all the footsteps leading up to it or all the little paths leading off it before you reach your destination. You have to walk that road and work out your own life whether you know the future or not.

When people find they have to take the steps themselves, or start going up one of those side-paths, they may think: This is nothing like the clairvoyance I was given! Then, perhaps two years later, they'll ring up to say: 'You'll never guess what's happened! Everything has turned out exactly as forecast!'

You also get the sceptics, who, rather than sit back and wait, go and do the opposite of what the medium has recommended! One of these is a publisher friend called John: over a period of two or three years he asked me regularly for clairvoyance, and then deliberately went against any advice I gave him. This was partly because he didn't want his decision-making influenced by anyone else, partly as an experiment to see whether his behaviour would alter the outcome. In fact it never did; what I predicted always happened!

This gift is part of my personality, and there's no question of switching it on and off. It can arrive at any time and any place. I can be sitting at dinner enjoying the conversation, and suddenly I am given information concerning one of the guests. When clairvoyance arrives spontaneously like this, it is usually for a purpose. Sometimes it is to convince the unconvinced. Because of the nature of Alan's work, we often entertain; at one dinner-party I told an overseas client, who was rather sceptical about my work, that his right-hand man would leave him within three months. He said this was most unlikely; his colleague had been with him for twelve years. About three weeks later he phoned Alan to say that the man had given notice.

Usually the purpose of spontaneous clairvoyance is to comfort and reassure someone who is anxious or under stress. I also feel that when it comes unsought it is much more reliable than it might be if I were giving sittings for hour after hour. Mediums often have to interpret the information they receive; if they are unwell or tired, there is a risk of their giving an incorrect interpretation. The well-being of the client must always be uppermost in the clairvoyant's mind; I always make sure that what I give to others has come to me so clearly that I can't be mistaken.

My friend Louise received very detailed spontaneous clairvoyance on her first visit to me for healing, which was also our first meeting. She had just embarked on a second marriage and in the autumn of 1983 she and her husband, anxious to start a new home together, had started looking for a country cottage in Oxfordshire.

However, I immediately saw that they would be moving to Sussex, where they would be near a commuter line. (Louise has to travel to London for her work.) Accordingly, the couple began house-hunting in Sussex. At first they had no luck, but on her next visit I was still certain that Sussex was where they would find their dream cottage. The clarity of the pictures given to me was amazing; I could see the South Downs and the surrounding countryside as if I were there.

And I had further information for Louise. 'Although you can go on looking,' I said, 'the cottage will in fact find you.' I described it to her as I saw it: 'It has hills in the distance, it's surrounded by trees and there is some sort of pond adjacent to it. Although there is a large house next to it, I don't think you will be able to afford that one. The cottage is not free at the moment, but you will be in it by next summer.'

Within a week, Louise had received a phone call from her sister to say that her husband's uncle had just died, leaving everything to his sister. The property included a big house in Sussex which had been sold, and a cottage next door which the sister was thinking of selling. Louise asked me to go and see it with them; before we set out she showed me a photograph of the cottage. I said: 'Yes, this is the house I saw. It belongs to a woman who has only about three weeks to live.'

When we drove down there it was just as I had seen it: a charming rosy brick cottage, next to a large, beautiful but dilapidated house – which the couple could certainly not have afforded! It was in a country area, but near a commuter line. The garden, which included a sunken lawn, was bordered by trees and had an uninterrupted view of the South Downs at one end – all exactly as I had seen it. But I was puzzled. I told Louise: 'This is just what I saw, but there is no water. I know there was water.'

The new owner was very ill and was in fact to die within a month, but before then Louise and her husband took me to meet her, along with a young cousin. While I gave the sick woman some healing to relieve her pain, Louise and her husband walked in the garden with the cousin. He suddenly burst out in an embarrassed way: 'There's one thing I ought to have told you about the house. When my uncle bought it, there was a pond where the sunken lawn is, so it may be very damp!'

That was obviously where I had seen the water. Could the previous owner have been giving me the information and showing me the scene as he had seen it the first time? He had obviously loved the place, and I feel sure that he wanted the next owners to love it, too. Louise tells me that the house, with its calm beauty and ancient atmosphere, feels very important to them both; it has not only given them roots, but is also a source of inspiration to her husband, who is a writer.

The actual purchase was dragged out by legal complications and the sale of Louise's London house, but in August 1984 they finally moved in. A curious and pleasant postscript to the story is that not long afterwards Alan and I moved to our present home, which is ten minutes' walk away!

After their move, Louise wrote to me: 'During all this doubt and worry, the power of your clairvoyance and the accuracy in detail after detail and your assurance that we would eventually live in the cottage kept our spirits and determination going.'

However, knowing it's all going to come right in the end doesn't mean that you can stop making an effort.

Another potential misuse of clairvoyance is when clients simply want decision-making taken out of their hands, which isn't good for anyone. Sometimes I've asked these people, 'What do you want out of life?' and received the answer, 'I want someone to tell me.' But we were all given minds with which to plan our own lives. Most people know at heart what they would like to achieve: the best help you can give yourself is to visualize your goal in your mind and work steadily towards it.

It is your life, and there is always a choice. If you can train yourself to have 'clear vision' by being positive and independent and working hard for your ultimate goals, you hold your fate in your own hands. It's always best to try to make positive decisions for yourself, and only seek clairvoyance when the situation is confused.

One situation I have learned to avoid is giving clairvoyance to both partners in a troubled relationship. The clairvoyant can only too easily be used as a scapegoat; each partner can bring out information given in confidence and use it as a weapon against the other, instead of taking responsibility for their own feelings and opinions.

Clairvoyance is very useful for surveying houses! If I am given an address, I can immediately list any existing problems. Only recently I did this for a friend: I could see that among other things there were two defective slates and a cracked gutter, although the builders were supposed to have completed the roof. They were sent back to have another look, and this time they found them! I have detected faulty damp courses which have eluded the surveyor, and I can also tell whether there is a bad atmosphere, or whether the neighbours are likely to be difficult – all extremely useful to anyone before buying a house.

One young couple came to me about six years ago; they were interested in a house, but the price was suspiciously low, and there seemed to be a great deal of secrecy concerning the previous tenants. I was able to tell them that the previous tenants had suffered serious health problems because the house was built above a stream. Underground streams, however deep, usually have an adverse effect on health, and I advised the couple not to buy. They took my advice; later, the existence of the stream was confirmed by a well-known dowser.

Another helpful clairvoyant gift is my ability, on being given a name, to describe the owner's character: it is as though someone shows me a file with all the relevant information in it. I can't remember how many thousands of names I have been given over the years, but the detailed summing-up I receive always turns out to be accurate. I am often asked how this can be, when so many people have the same name: I can only assume that someone who is aware of the person concerned is responsible for beaming the information to me.

When Alan was about to visit Hong Kong for the first time, he made some appointments in advance. He gave me the names of three Chinese contacts he was to meet, and I wrote down the clairvoyant information I was given about them – they were all three totally different. He phoned me a week later to say I had been right about them all. He still used his own judgement, as he always does, but this extra knowledge reinforced his confidence.

Clairvoyance can be an incredible business asset as it helps people to keep one step ahead; I have helped many professional men and women in this way. Obviously, it should only be used ethically. It might be possible to use it for self-seeking motives, but anyone thinking of doing so should bear in mind a very important spiritual law: What you give out you get back. A medium or anyone else who used clairvoyance for the wrong purposes would certainly find it rebounding on him in some unpleasant way! In fact much of the business-orientated clairvoyance I have given has been to protect the innocent.

There was the young woman whom I told not to accept an appointment as company secretary and never to sign anything for her boss, which he was trying to persuade her to do. I could see that if she agreed she would eventually be liable for heavy costs as there were some unsavoury things happening within her firm. She took my advice and later told me that I had been absolutely right!

I was also able to help a young man through what must have been the worst period of his life. He had become involved with some men who were highly experienced in dubious financial wheeling and dealing. He visited me regularly for two years, during which I was able to tell him who he could trust and who he couldn't, and foresaw every single twist and turn his enemies were about to perform. Consequently, he was ready to cope with each situation as it arose, and was never caught out. There was no doubt that this foreknowledge saved him from going to prison for other people's misdemeanours.

* * *

Probably the most satisfying use of clairvoyance is when my gifts can provide guidance to people who are genuinely seeking the right path and are willing to put in some effort. Take Andrew, for example, a young man who came to visit me in March 1985.

After graduating in oriental languages, Andrew had just spent six months working for a computer company in London, where his talents were not properly employed; he felt he was in a rut, and was quite despairing. We had met once socially, and he thought I might be able to help him. He was also very keen to give up smoking, a habit he'd been trying to break for some years, and knew I'd been successful in treating this with hypnosis.

I took him into my healing-room and after a brief chat asked him to sit down quietly. I immediately began receiving information about him from his paternal grandfather. I described the grandfather, very accurately according to Andrew; I told him that he'd come to help him, and was actually looking after him and guiding him all the time.

I assured him that he mustn't worry about his career, since his future was being taken care of. He would shortly be offered a new job which would take him to the Far East, where he had already spent some time studying. More important, the move would introduce him to some high-powered and influential people, who would be of great help when he came to fulfil his destiny.

I knew that he was on a spiritual path, and would eventually help other people. I told him about some of his previous lives, which he had shared with his wife, and reassured him that there were people looking after him and channelling him in the right direction.

Our talk continued for a long time, and Andrew was so overwhelmed by all I told him that he forgot to ask for hypnotherapy. In a recent letter to me, he comments: 'I cannot really adequately describe the feelings of tremendous inner peace and well-being I felt after my visit. I had felt at a very low ebb, but after leaving, a profound feeling of relief and happiness.'

The fact that Andrew's future was already planned out for him didn't mean that it was all made easy. As he says, 'You're pointed in a certain direction, and then it's up to you.'

It happened that he had already been interviewed by a company which was considering opening up a branch in Singapore, but had heard no more from them. Shortly after his visit to me, they asked him to prepare a proposal about why and how they should set up a Far Eastern branch. He prepared the proposal, which involved a good deal of work, and again heard nothing for some time.

After a six-week wait, he telephoned them because the firm he was with was going through major changes, and he felt it would not be right to take part in these if he was leaving. This time his proposal was accepted, and he was offered a three-month trial period to set up the headquarters in Singapore. He achieved this successfully in August 1986, and has been working there happily ever since. He has since written to me that he has met the important people I told him of, and 'everything you forecast has come true.'

Incidentally, I saw Andrew several times for healing after that first visit; he was still failing to beat his smoking habit on his own, and the following June I gave hypnotherapy for this. Since then, he has never wanted to smoke.

As for his spiritual path, he says he would describe himself as 'a very ethical businessman', and feels that the experience he is gaining now is in some way preparing him for a future in which his talents will be of use to others.

It always surprises me when people ask me about my religion. Healers and mediums belong to all sorts of religion, but healing is a beautiful *spiritual* experience. To me there is an important distinction. Religion is a man-made concept, with sets of rules based on the Bible or other religious books. Spirituality is your spontaneous reaction to life: if you are a loving and compassionate person, you won't need rules to stop you from doing wrong or harmful actions; you will simply not want to.

Truly spiritual people are those who have lived and learned through many lifetimes, and have acquired love and compassion as their minds have expanded. There are levels and degrees of spirituality, according to how far your mind has progressed. Spiritually progressed people do not need to be guided by religious dogma; in fact I find that they have a code of honour and a tolerance that I don't always see practised by some people who regard themselves as religious!

We all have a perfect right to believe what we wish according to our spiritual awareness. What we haven't the right to do is to impose our ideas on others or crucify them if their beliefs differ from ours. We all have different paths and we should follow the one that brings the most peace and satisfaction to ourselves. So I always advise people to listen to what others say, ignore it if they wish, but never ridicule them.

What is most important to my spiritual beliefs is the certainty that we continue living after death. Like all forms of energy, mind energy is indestructible; therefore the mind *cannot* die. Only the brain, which is matter, dies. I have seen mind energy leaving the dying, and I am convinced that this is the part of them that lives on – the spirit in fact. The mind simply moves into another dimension where it is free from its limiting physical counterpart; it is able to help with healing and to communicate through mediums.

It is a great pity that something so wonderful should appear to many people to be fearful. The people who want to communicate are the friends or relatives they loved while they were alive, and their personalities are still exactly the same. But in the dimension they now occupy they are able to see much more clearly and further ahead; no longer locked in a time-capsule, as we are on earth, they are able to warn us or guide us, and if linked to us by love can also share in our joys or anxieties. (I believe that we ourselves escape from being time-bound by leaving our bodies in our sleep. That is why some dreams are predictive, and also why, when we go to sleep with a problem, we often wake up with the answer.)

In both this dimension and the next, we learn lessons which help us to progress. Most of us go through many reincarnations, each one with a specific purpose. As we progress through numerous journeys of enlightenment our spirituality hopefully increases, and as the mind expands the mind energy becomes finer and finer. Most of us around today are on a low-to-middle rung of the ladder; only a few people in this dimension are truly progressed spirits.

In this sense, I don't think that most healers and mediums are terribly 'spiritual'. What all mediums have in common is that they have expansive mind energies, which can reach out and touch into the next dimension, and are capable of acting as receivers through which the 'dead' can communicate, in mind-to-mind contact. I get rather annoyed when people expect mediums to be 'holier than thou'. They need to be down to earth, or they would lose their human touch and their ability to cope with the very earthly problems they confront, both during their development and daily in their work. Compassion is more important than either intellect or an oversensitive 'holiness'. All good mediums are people who are willing to serve and help others by passing on messages from the dead. This activity, incidentally, expands the mind further.

There are people who disapprove of efforts to contact the 'dead'. I have never tried to contact the dead. They are so busy contacting me that I am usually relieved to have a break! Over centuries the minds of the deceased have been trying desperately to prove to the living that there is survival after death. Accepting this message would remove the fear of dying and make our present lives far happier.

There is no doubt in my mind that I have been taught by unseen people all my life. I have been persuaded to seek knowledge and discouraged from wasting time. When I have ignored their advice, my way has been blocked, and nothing goes right until I am on the right path again. It is through this guidance that I have learned about mind energy, and that the mind and the personality survive the death of the physical body.

One question I have been asked time after time is whether there isn't a danger of evil minds communicating. Let me put that fear to rest for good. There is no chance of attracting a 'nasty' if you visit a genuine and positive-minded medium or healer. Someone who is working continually to alleviate suffering can only attract like minds.

I know that I have been taught by the finest teachers, and one lesson has been repeated again and again. There is a universal law that dictates that *whatever we give out will be returned in full*, often many times over. I have also been taught that love unites, hate destroys. Love and compassion are the link to the power that manifests through a good medium or healer. Love in its purest form is the *ultimate* energy.

Healers and mediums absorb knowledge all the time, and it can come in a variety of ways. Sometimes a voice speaks clearly to me while I'm occupied with something like washing up. At other times information is impressed on my mind less directly, particularly if my mind is in another dimension, as it is when I'm healing. The realization of what I have been given will come later: I may be writing or meditating when a fascinating idea will come to the surface. (My editor says it sounds like putting a programmed disk into a word processor; all the information is on it, but you can't read it until you switch on and bring it up on the screen!)

It is often suggested that survival evidence is obtained through telepathic communication between the sitter and the medium. I have tested this theory time and time again; it is certainly possible for some basic information to be picked up in this way, but the quality of a genuine communication is quite unmistakable. As you will see from the stories in the next chapter, it is quite usual for evidence to be given which can only be confirmed much later on, when more information has come to light.

Telepathy is really the ability to alter your mental wavelength, enabling you to attune to another mind. My ability to communicate with the minds of other species is purely telepathic. Some people can cultivate and practise telepathy, but more often than not it occurs by chance – most people have had the experience of 'knowing' when a friend was about to ring.

Thought is vibration, therefore mind interaction is invariably 'like to like': only minds with the same vibrational frequencies can communicate with each other. Minds with differing vibrations would be unable to do so. This is why, incidentally, some people will find themselves getting better survival evidence from one medium than from another, who in turn may give brilliant evidence to someone else. (Another reason why not all mediums are brilliant all the time is that there is a great demand for their services. It is so easy to fall into the trap of overworking and, as in any job, when fatigue creeps in, talent – psychic or otherwise – suffers.)

My psychic talents have for years brought peace, happiness and hope to people, not through any knowledge of mine but from those, now deceased, who have communicated through me. I have seen people transformed in minutes as I pass on information which only they could possibly identify with. Details of names, addresses and past experiences leave them in no doubt who the messages are from.

I have seen spirits standing or sitting beside people in restaurants, pubs, trains, buses, airports – in fact just about everywhere! I don't have to be very quiet or create a special atmosphere. If you are totally psychic, there is no need at all for dim lights and hushed surroundings. I also find that evidence given in everyday settings is often more easily accepted by people who might be too sceptical, or too scared, to visit a medium.

When I was living in Sutton, the telephone rang constantly with requests for absent healing. It was fascinating how spirit people used to appear as soon as I answered the phone. Sometimes it was quite unnerving for the person at the other end when I told them I had a deceased relative or friend standing beside me who wanted to communicate with them. The evidence was often so detailed that it would go on for an hour. Spirit people still arrive when people telephone me, but these days I no longer have the time to continue at such length.

The first time I saw a spirit actually waiting for someone to arrive, I walked into my healing-room and was surprised to see a shadowy woman sitting in one of the chairs. She sat looking straight ahead of her, as if expecting someone, so I left her alone.

When my next caller arrived a few minutes later, she looked exactly like a younger version of the presence in the healing-room, and I told her I thought her mother was waiting for her. When we went in the spirit was no longer visible, but she immediately began communicating with her daughter through me. In order to materialize, spirits have to make use of the energies available; then, when they want to communicate, they generally disappear from view since there may not be enough energy to do both. To project themselves into this dimension both visibly and audibly requires a tremendous effort.

For an hour my patient's mother talked about their family, giving names and addresses, and messages for family members. Some of the information meant nothing to my sitter; this quite often happens, but when I ask the person to check it out with other relatives the meaning always becomes clear. As this young woman was leaving I asked whether she and her mother had looked alike; she laughed and told me they had always been mistaken for each other. Then she thanked me profusely; knowing for certain that her mother had survived the death of the physical body had made her feel quite differently about life.

Since then I have had countless similar experiences. I can't recall how many times I have been told, 'You have changed my life' – always, I am happy to add, for the better. So many minds are trying to change all our lives for our benefit; for thousands of years they have been desperately trying to prove the survival of the mind. Yet we still doubt.

The dead have various ways of contacting us. A very common phenomenon is the healing-room being suddenly filled with the most beautiful fragrance, usually the favourite perfume of a relative who has chosen this way to identify herself. Another method with which I am experimenting is through tape-recordings. Despite the regular interference, I still record whilst healing because sometimes interesting things happen.

Once when we played a tape back we could hear the sound of coughing. The person with me identified it as his father, who had died of emphysema; he said he could never forget that sound. I've never – so far – recorded the voices of spirit helpers. However, on one occasion a friend brought a brand-new tape which we recorded on while healing. On playing it back we were very moved when we heard the most exquisite music; sadly, the next time we put it on the music had completely disappeared.

I experiment with tapes all the time; most of the results have been mediocre so far, but I am convinced that at some time the voices of the so-called deceased will use this method of communication. I have also done some experiments on the interference with a well-known physicist. He told me that the sound is called 'white noise'; it seems that the energies around me are affecting every known wavelength. Once when we were in the middle of recording a voice called out 'Hey!' in a rather comic-sounding Cockney accent, startling us both. The house was perfectly quiet both inside and out; his wife was also present in the house, and we all agreed that the voice could not have come from outside.

Some minds choose quite comical methods of communicating! Indeed, since practising as a professional medium I have enjoyed more humour in my life than ever before. This might seem odd to anyone who believes that communicating with the dead should be a serious and solemn affair. But you can't be miserable when the so-called 'dead' are as hilarious as they were in real life.

I don't think the communicator in the following story was intending to be funny, but we've laughed a lot about it since. My friend Fred is an electrician, and worked in partnership with his father-in-law before the latter's death. Very early in my healing career, his wife Shirley asked me to give hand-analysis sessions to herself and a friend. (I was still at the stage when I didn't quite trust my powers of mediumship and was using the hand as a focus.)

On the night they arrived I asked Shirley to sit downstairs whilst her friend Margaret and I went up to the small room I used when I wanted to be peaceful. When we returned Shirley said: 'You poor thing, what terrible neighbours you've got! All the time you were upstairs someone was jumping on the floor with hob-nailed boots!'

I looked at her in astonishment. Our Sutton flat was built like a castle, solid as a rock, and the first few months of frantic phenomena had stopped. Margaret and I had heard nothing. 'Perhaps it was the pigeons,' I suggested. Shirley looked at me disbelievingly. Before her session we looked through all the upstairs rooms, but found nothing unusual.

During Shirley's reading, without realizing what I was doing I let go of her hand and said: 'Your father-in-law is saying that when rewiring factories Fred should attach a piece of string to an electric cable and tie it to a mouse's tail; put a piece of cheese at the far end and it will be easy for the mouse to pull a new wire through the conduit.' It sounded so nonsensical that Shirley and I looked at each other and burst out laughing. I said: 'I'm sorry about that. I expect he was just pulling our leg.'

When we finally went downstairs, Margaret was as white as a sheet. 'I've heard it as well – just like someone with hob-nailed boots jumping on the floor. What on earth is it?' I was as puzzled as they were. It was quite different from the sort of phenomenon I normally experienced – somehow much more earthy and physical.

Shirley rang me next day to say that she had given Fred

his father's message while they were in bed, and he was flabbergasted. On their last job together his father had said: 'What we need in this business is to put a piece of cheese at the far end, and attach the electric cable to a pet mouse's tail and run it through!' Fred tells me that since then an electrical gadget called a 'mouse' has actually been invented to do just this.

Then, just when Fred had decided it was time for sleep, Shirley mentioned the noise that had puzzled us all. This was almost too much for Fred, who went quite white. He told Shirley that before his father did any electrical job in a house he would always jump on the floor to see how safe it was. What's more, he always wore boots, which made an awful noise. Fred was quite shaken and didn't want to know any more.

But Shirley and I always have to laugh when we recall that evening, and the spirit who leaped around in hob-nailed boots!

Fred and Shirley have received a lot of healing and clairvoyance from me. At one time when Fred was coming regularly for healing his father made contact at every session. Through me, he gave Fred the names of people who would offer him contracts, together with the exact nature and value of each one. He was always right; it became a weekly occurrence for Shirley to ring me to say that, once again, confirmation had been received.

Fred never quite got used to these communications! But it was his father's way of giving help when it was most needed, and a perfect example of how, even after death, people who care for us can give us not only love but also very practical assistance.

There are thousands of people walking the streets today who have had wonderful survival evidence but are too afraid of what people might think to talk about it openly. It is rather like an underground movement, unseen and unheard until there is an explosion. Perhaps this book will help light a fuse.

FOUR

The Survival of the Mind

> He who sees this does not see death;
> He sees neither illness nor suffering.
> He who sees this sees all that is,
> He attains everything everywhere.
> *Chandogya Upanishad*, VII, 26, 2

In 1985 a young man lost his ex-wife and children in a particularly horrific fashion. The story, with all the ingredients of a murder mystery, grabbed the newspaper headlines. For the bereaved young man, this was real life and not a thriller. By the time he contacted me a year later, although someone had been accused, the mystery, as far as he was concerned, was still unsolved. He had been through an enormous amount of anguish and was nearly cracking up.

Although he had never been interested in spiritual matters before, from the moment of the tragedy itself all kinds of odd things started happening, and from time to time he would feel tremendously peaceful and supported; curious coincidences seemed to be pointing to some meaning in it all. Despite this he had reached a point of near-collapse when a friend lent him Michael Bentine's autobiographical book *The Door Marked Summer*.

The book made him think, and wanting to understand more he wrote to Michael telling him something about himself and asking how he could contact a reliable medium – he knew nothing of mediums and couldn't afford emotionally or financially to come across a charlatan.

Michael gave him two names, one of them mine, and said: 'Don't tell me anything else about yourself, because the less I know, the more value there will be in what the medium will tell you.' Although I lived relatively far away, there was apparently something about the name Shine that appealed to him. In the summer of 1986, some three months after reading Michael's book, he telephoned me.

All he told me about himself was that his first name was Colin. Immediately, I got a strong impression and said: 'My God, your nervous system is in tatters! It's shot to pieces! Did you have a nervous breakdown two or three months ago, or come close to one?' He agreed that he had – though he hadn't thought that his voice betrayed the fact – but that he felt a lot calmer now.

I went on: 'You need healing yourself, but I can give you absent healing. You have a good friend with you, who's with you the whole time, and he's sort of looking after you.'

Colin, thinking of a pal who had been staying with him to keep an eye on him, said: 'Yes, that's right.'

'And he died in a road accident about three years ago.'

'*What?*'

'He seems to have been with you for the last eight months. Does that ring any bells? He's someone you had a very good rapport with.' Colin immediately remembered that eight months ago he had heard of the death of a good friend he had once worked with, who had been killed on a motorbike about two years earlier. Suddenly he began to understand why everything around him was beginning to fall into place.

While we were still on the telephone I received a great deal of clairvoyant information which I passed on to him. I told him: 'Your friend is saying that the project you are working on is very, very important, and you may have to go out on a limb over it.'

Colin was very impressed by this, as it wasn't a phrase he had heard used much, but he *had* just read Shirley

Maclaine's book *Out on a Limb*! I didn't know it, but he was writing a book about his experiences, partly as therapy, and partly in order to tell the truth to the public. By the time we ended the conversation he was already convinced that I wasn't a charlatan. But there was a great deal more to come when he visited me the following week.

Colin was a pleasant, nice-looking man in his early thirties; I still had no idea who he was. I took him into my healing-room, and we immediately picked up where we had left off. He had brought a tape with him, and we tape-recorded the session. As usual, there were terrible disturbances on the recording, but it was audible enough for him to type up a transcript afterwards. He noticed that the interference became worse as more people came through – and plenty of people came through!

Straight away, I got the impression of a terrible tragedy. When I receive this kind of survival evidence I feel awful: my stomach tightens up as if I were sharing in the fear, and I can feel affected for days afterwards.

'Does this involve your two children?' I asked. 'And your ex-wife?'

Colin, looking rather amazed, nodded agreement.

I went on: 'There were two or three other people involved. I don't know who they are at the moment. Older people. There were two men and a woman . . .'

Colin just stared at me. I suppose he hadn't expected me to pick up his situation in quite such accurate detail.

Then I heard the voices of two little boys, one of whom sounded older than the other. They sounded happy and were laughing. I described them to Colin. He told me that they were actually six-year-old twins, but that one did sound older; the second one cultivated a babyish voice because he was the younger by a few minutes. A little later, I heard this younger voice saying: 'You'll know that I'm Nicholas.' That, said Colin, was what he always used to say, to make sure he wasn't muddled up with his brother Daniel. Daniel never felt the need to make that distinction.

Then an older man came through; I described his personality, and Colin recognized it as his father-in-law. This man was very angry about something; I told Colin that the man himself would have to deal with it. This bothered Colin, because it seemed to be something over and above the terrible events, and he couldn't understand what it was. (Now he does, and the reason will probably be made public in due course.) The man now started shouting about someone called David. 'Who's David?' I asked. 'This man is saying that David knows all the answers.'

'That'll be his nephew.'

'Well, David knows all the answers, and at some time or another David is going to have to tell you.'

At this point, knowing that David's evidence was important and also confidential, Colin made up his mind that I had given him enough survival evidence to convince him. He decided to tell me that his full name was Colin Caffell; it was his ex-wife Sheila, the model called 'Bambi', who had been murdered with their two children and her parents in a mass shooting at an Essex farmhouse the year before. Her brother Jeremy had by now been charged with the murders.

The police had told David Boutflour not to speak to anyone, including Colin, so no one at that time knew that David was the person who found a blood-stained silencer in the gun-cupboard, as well as other evidence showing that things had been set up to incriminate Sheila. Colin has been writing his own story, so I won't go into further detail about the shootings. But many of the things that I was able to tell him did not make sense until much later, some time after the trial.

Colin was simply glad to know that the twins were well and happy, and greatly comforted when he learned that they had made the transition in their sleep. I told him: 'They're laughing. Every time they come through, they are laughing.' Colin told me that was how they were in life; everything struck them as hilarious! 'Although it's tragic,'

I said, 'it's almost as though they made the transition so quickly they didn't have time to think about anything.'

'What about Sheila?' he asked. 'Did she know what happened?'

I said: 'Your wife has been put into a state of rest. She is being looked after.'

I was then given a great deal of information about Colin's work. 'Do you do sculpture?' I asked. He told me that he was a potter by profession, but had just started experimenting with sculpture; he was planning a sculpture of Sheila and the twins. I told him: 'It's not a gift you were born with; it's been given you for a purpose. A sculptor has attached himself to you for his own progression, and because he has the same vibrational rate as you. He's been given the job of helping you.' (At that time I couldn't give the sculptor's name, but later on when I spent an evening with Colin I was given the name of Rodin. And, later on still, another medium also told Colin that Rodin was working through him.)

I then told him that eventually that particular gift would leave him, once it had fulfilled its purpose. 'The last two sculptures you'll do will be of your children, because I can see them finished. Then that will be the finish of that part of your life. You will have paid a debt, as it were – not that you owe them anything, but it is your debt to yourself. It's almost as though the living minds of your children are going to enter these pieces.' I could also see that he had a gift as a writer, and that in future he would be helping people through writing and lecturing.

After our first session Colin felt greatly reassured. He checked over the tape and transcribed it; there were a few things he felt that I might have picked up telepathically, but overall he was convinced. He played the tape to a very sceptical friend of his, Brian, who had previously warned him against visiting 'occult types'. Brian was amazed at the transformation in him. 'So much light shone from him and still does,' he wrote afterwards. 'It was as though Betty had almost brought the people who were lost in the tragedy back to him. He was totally convinced they were well and happy.'

Brian, who is in the music business and was going through a bad time himself, decided to come to see me, too; he made an appointment without telling me of his connection with Colin. I was able to advise and help him; numerous people came through whom he could not fail to recognize, among them one of Colin's twins, Daniel. He reminded Brian that he used to sit on his shoulders to try to reach 'a big silver balloon in the air' in a place full of flashing lights. Brian recognized this as a mirror ball hung from the ceiling that Daniel had wanted to play with at one of their performances. He found this all the more convincing because only Daniel would sit on his shoulders. Nicholas considered it too babyish!

For the no longer sceptical Brian, the *coup de grâce* was when a little boy called Harry also came through, wanting to say 'Hi! and thanks for the chance to play the piano!' Brian was staggered; three years before he had been in a band that had played at the Royal Albert Hall. Harry was about twelve, a keen young pianist whose parents were friends of Brian. Before the performance Brian had invited him to come early for the sound check, and to have a look at the keyboard instruments. The band had let Harry play the Steinway grand piano for the sound engineer to set the test, and for ten minutes or so Harry had played the piano at the Albert Hall, pure happiness written all over his face. Harry had died tragically shortly before Brian's visit. But what he recalled was that happy occasion, not the sadness of his death.

Colin was quite satisfied with the evidence he had been given at our session, but he received even more when he joined us for dinner one evening shortly before Christmas. Once again the twins came through, still laughing and happy, and we all had to put down our knives and forks and listen to what they had to say! Interestingly, they mentioned that someone called Ollie was 'still sad'. Ollie was a friend of Colin who had taken his own life when the twins were quite small; the point of this message seemed to be that suicide is not an answer! I have also had many suicides who have come through quite quickly and have found peace of mind; clearly, it is we ourselves who eventually have to make the effort to progress.

Next, the twins told Colin not to forget to hang his Christmas bell again this year; they were referring to a Christmas wind-chime with a model Bambi attached to it, which hung on a rose-bush behind their grave. Colin didn't discover until his next visit to the cemetery that it had gone missing and had to be replaced – the twins were evidently there ahead of him. And then they told us: 'Mummy's back. She's awake. She's been to see us.' Later on, Sheila herself came through and sent a personal message to Colin.

Since that time, Colin has been growing and progressing as a person. He has been both sculpting and writing, has been to a number of workshops on healing and similar subjects, and visited the spiritual community of Findhorn. Above all, writing his own book has helped him to make sense of what must have seemed a total waste of so many lives.

Few lives are really wasted. I have included Colin's story at length because it contains so many of the things I teach: that the mind and the personality do not die, that we come here with a purpose, and that what we don't learn or fulfil in this life we carry on to the next. It also shows the value of mediumship and survival evidence.

In my experience people only receive information from the 'dead' when they are in need, or when there is a real purpose behind the communication. That's why people who visit mediums simply out of curiosity can be disappointed. The main purpose of survival evidence is to prove to those living in this dimension that the mind does not and cannot die; this explains why some messages from the 'dead' appear trivial to those not personally involved. Those unexciting messages concerned with small domestic details show that the communicators are still watching over the people they care about.

Many of my clients have told me that they never thought they would find themselves sitting talking with a medium or a healer: that they'd never been able to understand why others needed to seek such help. Nevertheless, there they were, sitting in my room, because they were in desperate need and could think of nobody else who could help them.

Probably the most common reason for the 'dead' wishing to communicate with their friends and relatives is simply to bring them peace of mind. This happened recently with my daughter Janet. She had a very close friend, a pupil at her yoga class called Annette. Long before she fell ill, she and Janet used to have deep conversations about life and death and what the afterlife would be like. Annette often used to say: 'If anything happens to me, I shall certainly come back and let you know.'

Annette had a lot of stress in her personal life, and at only forty-three she became riddled with cancer; even so, she managed during her last few months to be of great help to someone close to her who had severe problems. When she died, Janet was grief-stricken; knowing that your friends survive doesn't stop you missing them. One evening, while meditating, she thought: The person I'd most like to hear from is Annette.

It happened that the next day I had invited Charles Horrey – the medium who had originally told me I must be a healer – to lunch; I wanted to thank him and tell him how I'd been doing in the last thirteen years. Janet was not with us, and didn't even know he was coming. In the middle of the meal I was chatting to Charles when he said: 'Hang on, I must stop you, Betty, because I have Annette here.'

It was quite clearly Janet's friend, who told us that she was glad to be released from all her pain; that she was now totally happy and peaceful, and thrilled to find herself in a very beautiful place.

Janet was thrilled, too, when I told her about this; it

was just what she needed at that time. Although she herself has given some extraordinary survival evidence, and has often received it from me, it was the first time she had heard it from another medium. It is nice that it should have come through Charles Horrey!

Some people object that visiting mediums is a way to avoid going through the grieving process. This isn't my experience. Coping with the death of someone we have loved dearly, or even an acquaintance with whom we have spent time, is always difficult. What we are really suffering from, however, is our own selfishness. This is something we have to deal with throughout life, but death really brings it home to us. Of course it is normal to grieve. However, most people go to mediums a little while after a death when, like Colin and Janet, they have been through the grieving process and feel that enough is enough. When grief continues too long it is very unproductive. Learning that their loved ones are alive and happy releases people from their negative grief; they themselves can become happy and positive again, and get on with living.

If you think about it, death, whether through accident or through disease, occurs because of the breakdown of the physical body. When we cease to be healthy, and suffering goes on a long time, death is a gift. Therefore, we should be happy for those whose minds have been freed from pain. I have known some people who, knowing that a relative is going to die of a painful or debilitating disease, have been able to do their grieving beforehand. The grief is not suppressed, but when that person finally leaves them they are able to feel glad for and with them. This seems to me a very positive approach.

I don't believe in visiting mediums time and time again; this kind of obsession has given mediumship a bad name. If you want to keep in touch with someone and send them your love, you can always sit quietly and think about them. If people want to see me more than twice for survival evidence, I try quite firmly to dissuade them. I point out that it isn't healthy to go on living in the past, nor is it good for the person who has moved into the other dimension and needs to get on with life there. Mentally hanging on holds them imprisoned by your mind. If they come back later without being sought after, then it will be of their own free will and for a good reason, not because they feel obliged to keep reassuring the bereaved.

Children are perhaps the hardest of all to let go of; the death of a child is always tragic. When a mother or father receives evidence that their child is happy, and continuing to learn and grow, it can bring them enormous comfort and help them to let the child go. In fact bereaved parents are in constant touch with their children, did they but know it; the children are obviously aware of this even if the parents are not. Very often after a child has come through the mother will say: 'Isn't that strange – I've been dreaming about him!' I will explain that she has not been merely dreaming but has actually left her body during sleep to be reunited with the child. (This is also the case in many dreams about 'dead' friends and loved ones.)

In fact the mind is ageless, in the sense in which we understand ageing. But the spirit of a departed child will come through as a child, and will even continue growing up in the other dimension in order to show the mother that life continues after death. Colin's twins told us that when they first arrived they were being looked after by a relative. There are people in the other dimension who choose to help children; in Colin's case a woman came through whom he couldn't remember but who had had a strong connection with Colin's own childhood. Later he learned who she was, and that she had lost her own twins at birth. Now she belonged to a group whose task was to take care of children. She told us that the twins were very happy, and continuing their lives as they had here, each following his individual path.

Quite often people are truly liberated by death, especially if the mind has been trapped and is unable to express itself in an impaired body. One day I was giving healing to a young Australian when a young man came through; he told us that he had drowned in a pond near his home in Australia. He described his home and the surrounding countryside, and added that although he had been very happy on earth it was only now that his mind was free of his body that he knew what it was to be a whole person.

My client listened intently; he clearly knew who the young man was, and appeared very moved as the message went on. The speaker was insistent that he should relay his words to his mother in Australia, telling her how much he had loved her and thanking her for the love she had given him. At the end of this very touching piece of survival evidence my Australian friend told me that the communicator had been his brother, who in this life had suffered from Downs syndrome. Later, he told me that the message had indeed brought peace to their mother.

We do not stop learning after death; on the contrary, it is important to continue to progress spiritually, which includes making up for past mistakes or for any hurts we may have caused to others. It is not unusual for minds to come through to ask forgiveness for something they have done, or failed to do, during their lifetime.

One young woman, Jilly, was sitting with me when her father, who had died two weeks before, came through and begged for her forgiveness. 'There is nothing for him to feel guilty about,' she said, but he was adamant that there was, and that he was very unhappy about it. 'I changed my will,' he told her, 'but I promise you I will make it up to you somehow.'

About a week later Jilly learned that her father had left his entire estate to a woman he had just met, rendering his daughter homeless. She was heartbroken, though she was helped by recalling her father's promise.

Three years later, her paternal aunt died unexpectedly, leaving Jilly a small fortune, and telling her in a letter that she had felt it only right to leave her the money because she had been so wronged by her father. Coincidence? I don't think so. I have heard too many stories like this to believe they could all be coincidences. When people make promises in the other dimension, they keep them, and her father must have impressed his wishes on his sister. Incidentally, Jilly had not told her aunt, or anyone else, about her father's messages, knowing they would not have approved of her visiting a medium!

Sometimes a mind will come through simply to help someone they were fond of in life. Jean and her mother, Mrs G, had never visited a medium or a healer before. Although Jean came for healing, their beliefs about life after death were totally changed in one and a half hours.

Jean had been in a car accident in America, and specialists there and in Britain had advised her to have her spleen removed as she was bleeding internally. She wanted to avoid this if she could, and on the recommendation of a friend got in touch with me for healing. I'm glad to say she completely recovered after two healing sessions and no operation was necessary.

On her first visit she brought her mother with her, and it was to Mrs G that I suddenly found myself passing on advice concerning her finances. What I was given was so extraordinarily detailed and specific that I could hardly believe it myself. It was even more of a shock when the communicator told me who he was. In his lifetime he had been a very well known financier; there could have been no one in the world better able to advise on finance.

When I told Mrs G his name, I laughed because it seemed so incredible, but she looked at me seriously and told me that this man had been her greatest friend and had always advised her when he was alive. Her whole face was illuminated; she didn't need to tell me what happiness this contact had given her.

I had no idea who Jean and her mother were before they came to see me. There could have been no question of telepathic communication between us since the action advised by her unseen friend was not in her mind; in fact, she told me, she would never have thought of taking the course he recommended! I learned later that she had done as he suggested, and that it turned out extremely well.

In the last hundred years all kinds of mediums have made their appearance in this country – trance, physical and mental mediums, some of them of very high quality. Yet there are still closed-minded people who claim that at best they have nothing to offer and at worst they are charlatans. It is true that because psychic phenomena can't always be produced to order some mediums in the past became afraid of failing and being ridiculed, and decided to cheat a little. This was their downfall, and it did no service to their cause. All the wonderful things they had proved were discounted because someone with no understanding of mediumistic gifts had something to hang them with.

One of the most dramatic pieces of evidence I have ever witnessed was on the platform of a local spiritualist church-hall. This was early in my healing days, when I was still exploring the psychic field, and we were promised an evening of 'transfiguration'. I managed to persuade Janet to accompany me, which she did with great reluctance!

I had no idea what to expect. I had read about transfiguration and knew that it was a very rare gift, hardly ever seen. I set off for the meeting feeling quite excited, though armed with a great deal of scepticism. When we arrived the hall was packed with several hundred people; we found our seats and sat quietly for about ten minutes.

The medium's rather theatrical appearance on the platform caused quite a stir. When everyone had settled down she said some prayers and then explained what she was about to do: she would lean forward slightly with her hands cupped together, scoop up ectoplasm from around her and bring it to her face. From then on any spirit person wanting to make contact would form an image of his face over hers and would speak directly to people in the audience. I gathered he would use her vocal cords, though quite how I couldn't work out. In fact, during all these preliminaries, I was thinking to myself: What a lot of rubbish!

The audience sat hushed as she went through the process she had described. Suddenly, her face started to change. I sat glued to my chair. This was the most exciting evidence I had ever seen. Slowly, a new and quite different face began to build up – hairstyle, eyes, nose, mouth – until it became that of a middle-aged woman. As the medium turned this way and that, giving us a three-dimensional view, I could hardly believe my eyes. Then she spoke in a completely different voice, giving a name and address. 'It's my sister!' exclaimed someone in the audience. What followed was quite extraordinary: a two-way conversation between the 'dead' woman and her sister. When this was finished, the woman's face dissolved to be replaced by that of a man, topped by sleek black hair and even wearing a moustache. He was followed by an old man with a beard and glasses. Again the names were given; again recognition from people in the audience; again emotional reunions. I was too transfixed to listen to what was said. It was as though these people had actually returned to life.

Almost the last person to appear was an elderly lady with hair pulled back in a bun and with a lovely smile. Looking across in our direction, she said: 'You never thought you would see me, did you!'

The woman sitting next to me grabbed my arm and cried: 'My God, it's my mother!' Tears streamed down her face as her mother began to speak, and it took some time for me to persuade her to put her hand up so that the medium would know the lady had been recognized. Still clinging on to my arm, she answered her mother's questions. As this face finally dissolved she was still weeping with happiness. All my scepticism had taken a back seat.

Much more common than this extraordinary experience is trance mediumship in which the medium's mind moves out of the way to allow a spirit, very often a guide, to speak or heal through them. Very often the medium is unaware of what is going on during this time. I think spirit people are working through mediums and healers all the time, but some of them prefer to work directly in this way to ensure that they don't get misinterpreted.

Several times when I first started healing I felt my own face begin to change, and had a strong inclination to waft off. On one occasion I went along with it, and apparently spoke in the voice of a Norwegian man; I can't remember any of it myself. Janet found this very frightening, and as I always like to know what's going on I never allowed it to happen again. But I often find myself saying things that surprise me. Sometimes, when I've been giving a lecture, I've said afterwards to Janet: 'That was very interesting! I didn't know that!' Someone has obviously been speaking through me.

It is because of the continued existence of the mind that mediums can give a clear physical description of a person who is communicating, and the 'dead' can reproduce their features in transfiguration. The surviving mind, with the memory of its physical characteristics still intact, is able to project an image that is recognizable to the recipient.

Survival evidence also shows that whoever we are in life we continue to be when we find ourselves in the next dimension. We do not suddenly become all-powerful and all-knowing. I am often asked why communications contain so much detail about the departed person's everyday life. We have to keep things in perspective. For millions of people on this planet life is fairly undramatic and repetitive, a daily round of looking after or providing for the family, working, shopping, cooking, sleeping, with the occasional holidays and outings. So what is most deeply implanted in the mind are naturally the ordinary everyday things.

Nor does dying suddenly make us extremely holy! Let me give you an example. Alan first visited me for hypnotherapy to give up smoking. After the session had finished

I told him that someone called Jim had come through, saying they had played golf together. Alan knew at once who it was. Jim then said, through me: 'You never did get a hole in one, you old bugger!'

He was referring to a long-standing joke between them: Alan and Jim had had a bet on who would be the first one to get a hole in one. And there was no mistaking the form of address! On the face of it, this contact could seem rather frivolous, but that was exactly Jim's way. At the time Alan was in need of the reassurance that there is a life after death, and for Jim to speak as he always had answered that need.

Some people are shocked when the deceased come out with bad language, but these lively 'dead' can bring a lot of fun into the conversation. And how else should they speak? The personality survives death, and if someone had a sense of humour when alive it will still burst through undiminished during communication.

One day, I was giving healing to a woman when her brother Mike came through; he had been killed in a car accident two years earlier. For the next hour Mike regaled us with joke after joke; we spent the whole session laughing! My sitter commented that if he hadn't come through with jokes it wouldn't have been her brother!

Mike also had a more serious reason for communicating; he told us that he had been secretly engaged and had died before he could tell his family. During the following week his sister made a number of enquiries, and with the aid of the information Mike had given her she managed to trace his fiancée and broke the news of his death. The young woman said that Mike had never given her his home address; when she stopped hearing from him she assumed that she had been just a passing fancy, and had been too hurt to make extensive enquiries herself. This is another example of how, if something has been left undone, the 'dead' person will leave no stone unturned until he can make things right again.

With my life so busy, I never gave much thought to the

afterlife of animals until it was brought forcibly to my attention. I had been healing for about six years. I was working very hard and had had a particularly difficult day. As I sat relaxing in the evening I found myself in the other-dimensional garden that I still visit regularly. I was making my usual way along the path, when something landed on my shoulder. Perhaps I should explain that when I am in this garden the experience is quite real and physical; if I want to, I can touch objects and leaves, and feel them as solid.

This experience, however, was so *very* physical and so unexpected that it made me jump! Then I realized that it was my *cat*! There on my shoulder was the cat who had been put to sleep when I left Spain, purring and wrapping herself around my neck. It was a very emotional reunion and a very beautiful one as well as a reassuring experience. Ever since then, whenever I visit my garden, Sadie is always there to greet me. Sometimes she jumps on my shoulder; sometimes she just walks along beside me. I had grieved for her for a long time; now I have ceased to grieve.

I hope this will comfort others who have lost pets. Like people, animals continue to exist in another dimension, and are still drawn to the people who have loved them.

Much more attention is being paid these days to the process of dying. In the past the subject tended to be brushed under the carpet; nowadays there are counsellors in hospitals and hospices to help the dying on their journey into the next life. I feel sure that older people and the terminally ill – anyone, indeed, who fears death – could also receive a great deal of comfort from talks by mediums, who could prove to them beyond doubt that there is a life after this one.

I have often been asked to help relieve the pain of the terminally ill, and have also often had to tell relatives that the sick person will probably 'die' quite quickly. While healing can very often prolong life, it will speed up the process of dying if that is in the person's interests. When life is made intolerable through illness, healing helps to release the mind energy from the physical body.

Countless people close to death have conversed with spirit people who were waiting to accompany them on their journey. The joy on their faces when they have recognized their loved ones is indescribable. This phenomenon happens far too often to be ignored or passed off as the fantasy of a dying person.

Understanding that the mind *cannot* die can remove the fear of death once and for all. James was a dark-haired, gentle, good-looking young man, who never told me his surname. At only twenty-six, he was facing the fact that he was dying of leukaemia. I think his main reason for wanting to see me was to prepare himself for death by finding out all he could about the other dimension. I knew that there was nothing I could do as far as a cure was concerned; but healing always relieves pain and brings peace, so I saw him regularly for some months.

During his first appointment James's grandmother came through and, after confirming her identity by giving her name and describing her appearance, she went on to describe the house she had lived in and mentioned members of the family by name. She then gave a graphic account of the dimension in which she now found herself. In particular she emphasized how beautiful the colours were and how clean everything was! Finally, she gave a description of four members of the family and details of their careers which baffled James completely as he knew nothing about them. On his third visit, however, he told me he had found someone who did know them and that the descriptions he had been given were perfectly accurate.

He looked at me and said: 'For the first time since I learned I was going to die I have found peace. You have proved to me that there is a life after death.' He smiled, and went on: 'I shall have to improve my mind as quickly as possible. I've wasted so much of my time and I don't want to appear a moron to the people who have to cope with me when I arrive at my next destination.'

James lived for six months after this, considerably longer than his medical prognosis. During this short period he read everything he could about the universe and the collective mind, and when the time came he died peacefully. I know that his personality continues but, even so, I miss his physical presence. He had a lovely personality; in fact he was one of those people who seem almost too nice to be here. He always had a faraway look in his eyes, as though he had only decided to come here for a short time. I think that some souls come here only briefly for a particular purpose, and once this is accomplished they leave again peacefully. What James's was, I never knew. My clairvoyance only shows me what it is necessary for me to know, and we did not talk about it.

Dying can be a joyful and even exciting experience, and there is really nothing to fear. When we die, we are taken care of; there have been many accounts by people who have had near-death experiences, describing how they travelled down a tunnel at the end of which they came to a bright light and were greeted by someone who loved them. To people who find this far-fetched, I point out that dying is very like being born, which we have all experienced. When you come into this world, you travel through the birth canal and enter into a place where the lights are suddenly bright and people who love you are waiting to welcome you!

Many of those who have returned from a brush with death describe extraordinary experiences and visions, during a tantalizing glimpse into the unknown which many of them find all too brief. I believe this experience can be accounted for by shock dislodging the mind energy, enabling people to 'see' into the other dimension, just as mediums can.

No one is ever the same after a near-death experience. A new spirituality enters the very substance of their being, and their thought processes change totally. There can be no fear of dying, having once seen through our own dimension and tasted knowledge of the life beyond.

Death is far from being the end. It is a birth into a new kind of life, and into further spiritual progress. Heaven and hell are within us both here and after death, and it is up to us to decide which we prefer. There are a few people who do not progress, or progress only slowly. They include those who have lived really evil lives, and find it difficult to break the habit even after death! There are also people who are so materialistic that they become totally attached to their surroundings and never leave them. A woman whose pride in her home has become the entire focus of her life may want to remain near it. (That is one reason why houses are 'haunted'! Ghosts are the minds of people who don't want to move on; love, whether of a place or of a person, can also prevent someone from moving on.)

You cannot progress spiritually until you have let go and rejected materialistic values. I do not mean that we should all become hermits and give away all our possessions. It is more a question of attitude: of whether you own your possessions, or they own you! Material things will always keep you imprisoned, in this life and the next. I think that people who do not own a tremendous amount are the happiest; the people who are contented and peaceful within themselves, who have time to see, to feel, to be, and to have a spiritual relationship with nature.

Those who do move on report very similar experiences. It is fascinating when they communicate with descriptions of the next dimension. One young man came through and described what happened immediately after his death. He found himself standing high up on a mountain, just as if he'd been dropped by helicopter. He couldn't understand how he had got there, because he didn't realize that he was dead. Almost immediately he was approached by a man he recognized as his late uncle, who conveyed to him telepathically that he was now in the next dimension.

It seems that people find themselves in a variety of

locations much as they would do here when they are born, but they have certain features in common. This young man described the scenery around him as quite beautiful. Beyond the mountain on which he found himself on arrival, further mountain ranges and valleys lay misted by a blue haze. The temperature was like that of a pleasant English summer day but, although it was comfortably warm, there was no visible sun; this often seems to baffle people who find themselves in the other dimension! The grass looked and felt the same as earthly grass except for the vividness of the colour.

It was the colours that astounded him most; they were quite fantastic – just as they are in my other-dimensional garden. Time and again, people have given me similar descriptions, always commenting on the wonderful colours.

On arrival in the next dimension it seems that people are first of all taken care of, in whatever way may be necessary. When I first spoke with Colin Caffell his ex-wife was being looked after. At the time, I told Colin: 'She needs an awful lot of rest. I feel she's being looked after. When she eventually comes out of this peaceful rest and realizes what has happened, everything will be so beautiful that she will automatically accept it.' And, as we have seen, in due course Sheila was able to renew contact with her children and communicate with Colin.

Life in the next dimension has been beautifully described by an excellent medium, Bertha Harris, in her book *Traveller in Eternity*. Music and concerts play a large part in it, and it sounds very enjoyable! We also definitely go through some further learning while we are there. However, after a period there – probably lasting eighty to a hundred years, though it can be very much shorter – it seems most of us choose to be reborn. (You always have choices, whichever dimension you find yourself in.)

I feel, too, that people don't necessarily return to this planet, because there are other planets on which they can be reborn, many of them invisible to us because they are vibrating on a different frequency. The universe is infinite, filled with worlds within worlds within worlds! Some of these are on much higher vibrational levels than the earth; we come back here because we have not progressed far enough to qualify for these higher worlds.

For many years I have had impressed on me the fact that there is no such thing as empty space; the thought has fascinated me, but with no qualifications in physics I have been unable to follow it through. However, when I mentioned this to a valued friend, Professor E. R. Laithwaite of Imperial College, London, he was kind enough to send me the following extract by a physicist, which simplified things for me and seems to support my thinking:

Of all the constraints on Nature, the most far-reaching are imposed by space. For space itself has a structure that influences the shape of every existing thing.

The idea that space has structure may sound strange, since we usually think of space as a kind of nothingness that is the absence of structure. We think of space as the emptiness within an empty container, as the passive backdrop for the lively play of material things.

It turns out, however, that the backdrop, the all-pervading nothingness, is not so passive. The nothingness has an architecture that makes real demands on things. Every form, every pattern, every existing thing pays a price for its existence by conforming to the structural dictates of space.

. . . Since our brains and perceptual processes have evolved to suit our own space, we cannot visualize those other spaces, but we have devised self-consistent mathematical descriptions of them, and we have come to recognize that the spaces in the world of the very small, in the world of the fundamental particles, and in the world of the very large, at the scale of the universe as a whole, differ dramatically from the space in which we live.

(Peter S. Stevens, *The Patterns of Nature*, Penguin, 1977)

I hope this information will at the very least make you think about 'space'. After all, there is an awful lot of it which is *apparently* non-functional!

Before we return to this dimension, we decide to take on a specific task or fulfil a particular purpose. Knowing this can help us to make sense of seemingly terrible events. When I was talking with Colin Caffell I found myself telling him that everything that had been happening to him had happened for a purpose, and had unlocked a compassion in him that he didn't have before. I said: 'You were brought into this world not to do what you wanted to do but what you elected to do before you were born. . . You've been thrown into the cauldron because you were living your life for yourself, and somebody had to say: "You didn't come here for this, you came here for something totally different. You are being forced to find the path of knowledge."'

And that is exactly what he is doing now. Colin in fact had not been living an especially selfish life, but he had not been following his pre-chosen path. By the time he came to see me he was already back on the right path, but it was good for him to hear it confirmed, while knowing that his family were now peaceful and happy has given him the peace to continue.

Among the decisions we make before returning is to choose our parents, whom we will have known in previous lives. If you want to know more about this, do read Peter and Mary Harrison's book *Life Before Birth*, which contains the most fascinating descriptions by children who remember returning here from the next dimension.

Some of them recalled being pushed into a river and then being in 'Mummy's tummy'; when I read this I immediately connected it with the pool in my garden, where people were being bathed. I realized some time ago that it was a pool of energy – the same energy that I see around people – and this river, it seems, is also energy through which the mind is pushed in order to reach this dimension.

Apart from it making sense, many of my own experiences confirm my belief in reincarnation. For one thing, I have noticed that I am very rarely able to get survival evidence for old people. The parents of people in their seventies or eighties very rarely come through, in my experience. (My own mother now comes through less and less often.) And we certainly don't hear from our ancestors, although if they were still around in the other dimension they might well be interested in their great-great-great-grandchildren!

It seems to me obvious that people who have been dead for some time have moved on elsewhere, and I think it very likely that by now they are members of our particular circles on earth. Reincarnation also explains why we can dislike or fall in love with people at first sight. If our knees start shaking at the sight of a stranger, it is probably not a stranger at all; we are actually recognizing a previous very close relationship.

Very convincing to me, too, have been my experiences of regression to previous lifetimes. At the beginning of my professional career, while healing friends their faces would seem to blur and I would see a different face superimposed on theirs. I soon found that, if they continued to sit quietly, without any prompting from me they would then regress back in time to recall memories of a previous life. I would ask them questions about how they felt and what they saw, being careful not to put any ideas into their minds. What was fascinating was that I would simultaneously be receiving clairvoyant information which tallied with what they were telling me.

This happened very strikingly with Janet. We were sitting quietly together one day when I saw superimposed over her face the features of an obviously Spanish lady, with black hair and rather dark skin, looking very regal and composed. (Interestingly, Janet has always felt more at home in Spain than in England.) Janet began loosening her collar. I didn't tell her what I could see until afterwards, but when I asked how she felt she said: 'Oh, I'm so hot, I'm so hot!' I could see clairvoyantly that she was in a big house in South America, obviously part of a ranch as there were lots of horses around.

Janet's regression lasted about half an hour, and she repeatedly complained about the heat. She told me afterwards that she felt that she was the lady of a grand house, and she, too, had been aware of the horses. She remarked afterwards that she thought she'd been rather hard done by in this life. 'This is why I'm always so hard up,' she said. 'I had it all last time!'

These days I very rarely have the time to indulge in this fascinating experience solely out of interest. I know that some people can become addicted to exploring their past lives; on the whole I think we have enough to absorb our minds in dealing with the current one. However, when regressions occur spontaneously the information that comes out of them helps to explain certain aspects of our current personality.

Recently I was giving a sitting to a friend when suddenly I said: 'Just keep still, close your eyes, because I've got something here. I'll tell you about it later.' I could see her quite clearly wearing a milkmaid's cap and carrying a wooden yoke, and I also saw the house where she lived. Afterwards I told her that her employers, who owned the house, had treated her very well, but she had never married or had children. In this life, my friend desperately wanted children; having been denied them in a former life explains why she wanted them so badly.

I told her: 'I don't know why, but I'm being told that you're going back to your roots, somewhere in Devon, and when you get there you'll recognize everything. The house you are going to buy will have a mountain ash in the garden.'

She exclaimed: 'How fascinating, Betty. We're just moving down to Devon.' Afterwards she wrote to tell me that she had found and recognized the house where she'd lived as a milkmaid; and there was a mountain ash in their own garden.

The chief relevance of this kind of experience is that it helps us to understand better why we are like we are now; it also demonstrates that something in us is everlasting. That 'something' must be the mind, which carries from life to life things that have made an impact on it, such as the longing for a child.

One very interesting point is that, while people like to imagine themselves as former Cleopatras or Napoleons, what usually comes up is something that takes even me aback. I recently saw someone as a cripple who had cared for orphans during the last century; never in a million years would I have expected to see this woman as a cripple. Yet it explains why she, and others with similar past lives, feel compelled to help people in this life and sometimes feel quite annoyed with themselves when they can't say 'no' to requests for help! The inner knowledge of what it is to suffer has developed in them compassion for those who suffer in this life.

Sometimes, if a past-life memory is causing real trouble, regression can occur spontaneously as part of the healing process. Very early in my mediumship I was giving healing to a pleasant well-dressed woman when to my astonishment I began to see vivid pictures of a woman with greasy matted hair clutching an enormous knife as she crawled over cobblestones in what could have been a prison. Suddenly she plunged the knife into someone's back. Then, rather like a film, I saw a new picture in which she was devouring a loaf of bread. It was clear that she had killed someone to get that loaf, and in those days she would have been hanged for it.

I looked at this nice suburban lady and asked: 'Are you afraid of knives?'

'How did you know?'

'I'll tell you in a moment, but are you especially afraid of *big* knives?'

'Betty, I've never been able to pick up a carving-knife – my husband always has to carve the meat.'

'I think I've been given this picture as a healer to cure you of your fear.' I then told her what I had seen. She was rather appalled at first but, given the kind of person she is now, her former self seemed so incongruous that we had to laugh about it. (It's worth remembering, when you think things are going badly, that it's possible to laugh about a horrific event in a previous life! Knowing that we have had many lives can certainly put our present problems in perspective.) About five weeks later she rang me to say: 'Betty, I've got to thank you. I've completely lost my fear of knives.' Understanding where the fear originated enabled her to let go of that fear.

Not every soul chooses to reincarnate. The doctors who help me, the scientists from the past like Pasteur, must have made some kind of choice to help the world from the other dimension. Let me tell you another story.

A lady came to me for healing for terrible headaches caused by arthritis in the back of the neck. While I was healing her I told her that a man had come through who said he was her doctor.

She looked perplexed and said: 'I've never had any doctors as friends – I don't like them!'

The communicator, however, continued with his message. 'He's laughing,' I told her, 'and saying that the last time you came was about your daughter who had awful ear and gland trouble.'

She frowned, and asked me to describe the speaker.

'I'm sorry, I can't see him,' I said.

Suddenly in the corner of the room the figure of a man manifested.

'My God,' I said, 'it's Harry Edwards!'

The woman laughed. 'Of course! Now I understand! He *was* my family doctor, because I never went to anyone else!' She was thrilled. Needless to say, so was I. He went on to remind her of numerous incidents which she remembered. Afterwards, she and I talked together for about two hours exchanging stories about the great healer.

You may wonder why he didn't simply give his name straight away. I think the reason is that jokingly referring to himself as her 'family doctor' was much more convincing. Spirits often give clues rather than names; a fraudulent medium could easily say: 'I've got Harry Edwards here.' The real Harry Edwards pulled her leg, just as he did in real life. I think it is very likely that, as with doctors and scientists, great healers go on working from the other dimension, helping and guiding healers in this one. No experience is wasted, and what we learn the hard way in this life can be used in valuable service in the next.

Life does go on, and so do we as individuals. We exist for the purpose of progressing spiritually, in both this dimension and the next. Therefore, whatever level we are at on the spiritual ladder, it is important to strengthen and expand our minds in this dimension if we are to make any kind of impact in our future existences.

PART TWO

Healing

FIVE

You Don't Have to Live with It

> Having opened
> the door of hope
> I know my spirit
> will soar and
> untold wonders will
> be revealed.
>
> BETTY SHINE

People often ask what healing can cure. Since healing works on the energy counterpart and the mind energy it's not so much a question of curing specific diseases as of working on those energies and encouraging the person's positivity; healing then takes place naturally.

Over the years I have helped hundreds of people with all kinds of physical and emotional problems, and I could write for ever about the wonderful healings I have seen. However, for this chapter I have chosen just a few typical and not so typical cases which illustrate how healing can cure almost any complaint, provided the physical body has not deteriorated beyond repair. Some of these people have kindly written their own accounts, which I shall be quoting to give you an idea of their experiences of healing.

Numbers of people have been to see me after the medical profession had given up and they had virtually lost hope. One of these was Margery, who had reached the point where she was afraid of waking in the mornings. She had suffered appalling migraines for eight years and was having to spend at least one day a week in bed. At her hospital she'd been told that nothing could be done for her: she would just have to go home and 'live with' her constant pain and misery. Then someone she met at a function gave her my name. Although she was quite frightened by the idea of visiting me (like so many people, she had a 'spooky' image of healers), she was even more worried at the prospect of her pain continuing for ever. Next day she rang up for an appointment.

Margery duly arrived, a woman in her fifties, looking decidedly nervous. The first thing I did was to help her relax by giving her some healing, explaining what I was doing as I went along. I found that the cause of her migraines was a tremendous amount of arthritic calcium in the back of her neck which was pressing on vital nerves in her spine. I told her what I'd found and after fifteen minutes asked her to get up from the healing-couch and sit on a chair. Then I placed my hand on her neck – and as the calcium broke up there was such a loud bang that Margery thought I had broken her neck!

I explained that this was quite usual when I placed my hands on arthritic joints – except that this was a particularly loud bang! She was reassured enough to come back the following week for just one more healing session. After that she made a complete recovery, and it is now several years since her last migraine.

Another woman with a similar problem was a singer whom I shall call Veronica. I feel that she was led to me through the unseen helpers who work through healers; I have learned never to underestimate their power. (Sometimes people come to me in very curious ways; one was a woman who was sitting on a bus in agony with back-pain. A perfect stranger sitting next to her handed her a card and said: 'I think you ought to go and see this lady.' The woman was so surprised she just said: 'Oh, thank you.' The card had my name on it, but told her nothing about me; nevertheless she came and knocked at my door. When I opened it, she said: 'I was given this card. I don't know why I've come!' She soon discovered why when I gave her healing for her back.)

In Veronica's case, she had to go to Leeds to be given my address near her home in Surrey. She was up there recording a television show when she developed a severe tension headache, which is not unusual for performers under the glare of studio lighting. Her dresser suggested she had a massage by a fellow-worker; this young woman turned out to be a former client of mine who, like many others, had become a healer herself. She simply put her hands on the back of Veronica's neck, and the headache instantly disappeared. Since Veronica was only in Leeds for the show, she gave her my name as someone she could see on a regular basis.

When she first met me, Veronica was surprised and delighted to be told that I had been a singer, too; there was no need to explain to me the strains and stresses of her life, and she knew I wouldn't regard her as a 'neurotic theatrical'. She told me that she had been medically diagnosed as suffering from arthritis of the neck-joints; this kept her in constant pain, and limited her movements – very disabling for a singer. She was in agony whenever she hit a high note, and only daily pill-taking made her life bearable.

I was able to eliminate the arthritis completely in a few sessions, and I now see her about twice a year to 'top up' the healing energy and prevent a recurrence – something I recommend to everyone; it definitely keeps them healthy. 'Imagine,' writes Veronica, 'no more pain – no stiff neck – no pill-taking. It feels like a great concrete weight has been lifted off my head and I am floating on air. Even colours seem brighter after a visit to Betty.'

Veronica is now a personal friend and it's nice to think that because of healing she can continue to give pleasure to thousands of people through her art. Healing can deal very effectively with headaches and migraines caused by tension or arthritis, and – although I have not had enough cases to be categorical about it – I have found it to be equally effective with migraines associated with food allergies.

I believe that allergies to certain foods are caused by an imbalance in the body's biochemistry that makes people react against the food, rather than the food itself causing the imbalance; when healing restores the biochemical balance of the body, the allergic reaction disappears without necessitating any change of diet.

A slim fair-haired young woman knocked on my door one day, hardly able to speak as she was in the throes of a terrible asthmatic attack. I led her into my healing-room and without asking any questions immediately began to give her healing. After about twenty minutes she had recovered her breath enough to talk. She told me her name was Jessica; she had recently been told by her hospital, after some fifty or sixty tests, that she appeared to be allergic to everything. If she ate fruit, her mouth and face would swell up. The family's pet greyhound had to be kept outside, and even so she suffered almost non-stop from asthmatic attacks. In short, her life was a misery.

I studied the energies around her and could see that they were completely unbalanced. I offered to see her once a week, and after six weekly visits Jessica went on holiday to Corfu. From there she wrote to tell me that she was able to eat anything, even fruit, without any side-effects. After she got back, the greyhound was allowed back indoors! She had made a total recovery.

Jessica's energy counterpart had been so severely congested that it had simply gone from bad to worse. Nearly every major organ was compressed by negative energy, and many other vital parts of her body were unable to function. Healing eventually dislodged this congestion, so that her body started ticking over normally.

Miserable and disabling as allergic conditions are, some sceptics might dismiss these kinds of healing as 'psychosomatic' – the result of simply helping a tense person to relax, or the effect of suggestion on someone already predisposed to be cured. But not all cures can be explained

148

away so easily; I have found that healing can improve or completely eliminate some very serious physical conditions, in highly sceptical and un-suggestible people.

One of these was Jan. When she made her appointment she told me nothing about her problems or why she wanted to see me. In fact she was deeply troubled by a kidney disease which had been diagnosed in 1978. Her consultant was obviously loath to give a prognosis; he had hopes that her condition could be kept under control for five years with medication, but he also warned her that she should make provision in her home for the eventual installation of a dialysis machine. Not a nice forecast for an attractive intelligent professional woman still in her thirties!

At the time of her first visit to me she was on daily antibiotics, and had so far maintained a 'satisfactory level'. But she was very conscious that her condition was degenerative and that 'time could be running out'. She said nothing of this to me; she had decided, as sceptics often do, to adopt the attitude of 'Well, let's see what she can do!'

Jan arrived on a cold January day in 1982, feeling, she writes, 'more than a little apprehensive'.

A million thoughts raced through my mind. What was I doing, me – the ever sceptic, waiting at the doorway of a person I had never met? She was sure to be small, wizened and dressed in black. . . I almost turned away from the door. Fear, curiosity, call it what you will, held me there. I was to be so grateful for that split second decision.

The door was thrown open and I was faced with a blonde, curly-haired, definitely not wizened, smiling face. 'You must be Jan. Do come in.' My doubts and fears began to dissipate and feeling a little more relaxed, I went in.

When I asked Jan which particular psychic talent she required, she quickly answered, 'Clairvoyance,' thinking

149

this was safest. Her idea of 'this magical thing called faith healing', she told me later, conjured up pictures of cloaked bodies prancing around their victims in an almost pagan fashion!

I gave her what she confirmed was an accurate account of her life so far together with some forecasts for the future, which must remain private. At the same time, I received information about her kidneys and knew that she was in a very poor state of health indeed. I didn't wish to worry her too much, so I simply said: 'I do think you would benefit from healing. May I try?'

Jan seemed to like the idea, although she was still very sceptical and during the session asked me a lot of very probing questions. I answered them as well as I could, and she seemed satisfied with my explanation that healing is a psychic science involving the manipulation of energies. Probably even more convincing, however, was what she experienced herself.

> I was surprised as, whilst lying on the couch there was no more than what appeared to be the simple 'laying on of hands'. Gradually, I felt this burning sensation at the back of my throat, quite an unusual feeling, but one I had experienced before when having one of my many kidney tests. I was told by the doctor that I would experience this sensation as the dye travelled round my body. And here it was again, but this time it was the energy I could feel.

I could see that the energy around her left kidney was seriously depleted; however, I was able to tell her that her right kidney was doing its best to cope with the extra burden. My clairvoyant diagnosis turned out to be perfectly accurate: shortly afterwards Jan received the result of an earlier hospital test which confirmed what I'd seen.

I also knew clairvoyantly that she would recover completely, though her steady improvement was still thrilling for both of us. Jan came for six sessions over two months, reducing to one a month and then to one every two months; she was eventually able to come off all medication and to this day remains fit and well. She now sees me perhaps once a quarter for her 'top-up', to which we both look forward as we have become good friends. Jan now has total belief in healing and has sent a number of people to me.

It is encouraging to read that the medical profession is becoming more open-minded about healing; I hope it won't be too long before doctors regularly ask for the assistance of a healer when medicine is unable to produce a cure. So many patients are told to 'go home and live with it', or given gloomy prognoses. Yet there is now much evidence to show that healing can cure many of these 'hopeless' cases. If doctors and healers could work together, not only would there be far less physical and mental suffering, but also the National Health Service drugs bill could be substantially reduced!

When Anne Lamey came to see me she was in her early fifties, and had been suffering pain and embarrassment for over twenty years. In 1954 she went to the doctor with a terrible pain in her leg from her knee downwards; he diagnosed a strained muscle but offered no treatment, simply telling her to rest the leg. It was already swollen and became worse; she had to replace her size 6 shoes with size 7. When she asked for a second opinion, all that was suggested was that she wear an elastic stocking. The pain increased, spreading to the top of her leg; finally, after years of worry, the problem was diagnosed as thrombosis and then phlebitis, for which no treatment was offered.

Walking continued to be agony, and Anne could not even sit in comfort. She took other medical advice, but to no effect; the thrombosis remained for twenty-three years. As she worked in a health-food store she knew a lot about alternative therapies and tried vitamin and mineral supplements, but to no avail. Finally, a relative suggested she should try healing.

When she came to me in 1980 her leg was still swollen and extremely hard. Simply pressing the muscle caused bruising, and there was a huge black hollow where the tissue had deteriorated; it was almost gangrenous. I felt very sorry for her.

During the first healing I could feel quite curious sensations in her leg from the knee downwards; it was just as if the muscles and ligaments were jumping madly up and down as they returned to healthy life! Anne could feel it, too, as well as a tremendous heat. These odd muscle spasms happened every time she came to me. After the first healing, the tissues of her leg became softer, and from then on she improved steadily. She came for six weekly healings, and I then recommended her to visit me once a month.

Three months after the first healing session, Anne's leg began to fill out, hair began to grow again and the formerly blackened part was a healthy colour. Now, after eight years, it's difficult to see that she had anything wrong at all. Occasionally her leg aches if she has to stand for a long time, but she has no other symptoms. I see her now perhaps three times a year.

For twenty-five years Anne had been unable to wear dresses without being embarrassed about the state of her leg; now she wears them all the time. Only another woman would understand the happiness this has given her. Her whole outlook on life has changed to one of optimism.

I have worked with a number of athletes who, through healing, have been able to take up their sport again almost immediately after an injury. Terry, a young man in his twenties, had practically given up hope of finding a cure for an Achilles heel problem he had suffered from for months. When he first ruptured the tendon playing squash, a fellow-player who knew me begged him not to go to hospital, where they would put his leg in plaster for at least three months, but to come and see me instead.

Terry's family had actually been closely involved with healing for many years, and he was aware that it could succeed where conventional practice had failed; however, being rather sceptical he took no active part in it himself. He ignored his friend's advice and went to hospital.

Three months later the tendon ruptured again during physiotherapy exercises! This time he decided that he might as well see me, though on the Saturday when he arrived he was actually booked for an operation the following Monday. He was walking with a stick and in obvious agony. He writes:

> I visited Betty very much with the attitude that I had nothing to lose and a great deal to gain but I would say that I was still resigned to entering the clinic on the following Monday. But instead of spending another three months in plaster, which I would have done had they operated, I was up and walking in two days after one session with Betty of about forty minutes.
>
> After a short while I was able to move a previously immobile ankle and after a few days was up and walking again without aid. I could see and feel that there was a rapid improvement and this continued after returning to see Betty on several other occasions.
>
> Having experienced this apparently miraculous cure which conventional practice could in no way emulate there is no doubt in my mind that healers like Betty Shine have the ability to initiate a rapid healing process.

When Terry walked into his office that Monday, clearly out of pain when he should have been lying on an operating-table, his colleagues were totally mystified! In fact I estimate that my healing has cured about two hundred Achilles heel problems; they usually respond magnificently. The healing energy has excellent effects with muscles, ligaments and tendons. Of course, electro-magnetism is now being used medically with these types of problem; I can't help wondering whether the doctors have been influenced by healing as, although they are not identical, there is a close similarity between electricity and healing energy.

Another young man who has often come to see me with sports injuries is David, the footballer I mentioned in the last chapter. The first time he came he was in quite a bad state – yet another young person who had been told to live with his pain!

It started when he twisted his ankle and badly sprained two ligaments in his foot. A physiotherapist treated it with ice-packs, manipulation and ultrasound, and after two weeks David was pronounced fit to play again, though his ankle was still rather sore. A month later he sprained it again, this time tearing some tissue around the Achilles tendon. On the advice of friends he went to see another physiotherapist, who used the same methods as the previous one and sent him out to play again.

This performance was repeated regularly for the next four years! David saw a total of nine physiotherapists, all of whom temporarily eased the pain. However, as David was beginning to realize, none of them offered a cure for the weakness which was now affecting both ankles. In fact the best advice one could give him was to come to terms with pain and put up with it! David writes:

I put up with the pain for far too long, in fact it got to the stage when after two games at the weekend I was crippled, walking with a terrible limp. Before some games I had to warm up for half an hour before the kick-off to get some circulation into my feet. To conclude, at the age of twenty my feet and ankles were well and truly knackered. When it was suggested that I should try a healer called Betty Shine, I offered no objections because I was prepared to try anything.

On my first visit, Betty explained that the ligaments and muscles had taken such a battering that my main problem was one of circulation. She laid her hands on my legs and almost immediately, what I can only describe as an inner heat welled up in my legs. This heat seemed to ebb and flow like a tide inside me, giving me a hypnotic sensation of being somewhere else. After two visits I was completely cured!

Since that day I have visited Betty on dozens of occasions for all types of aches and pains, and have never been disappointed.

A good example of Betty's unique talent occurred when I received a kick in the groin during a game. A particularly eminent physiotherapist correctly diagnosed a slight hernia and fitted me up with a makeshift truss. He explained that I wouldn't be able to play for another month and that I should see him again next week in case the injury deteriorated.

The following night Betty was able to see me and successfully cured the hernia; I played again the following Saturday. When the physio did check me over again, he expressed confusion, but eventually decided he had been wrong because a hernia couldn't possibly heal in such a short time.

David has had some remarkable healings, including the manipulation I have already described, and 'other times my limbs would creak, groan and crack aloud as damaged ligaments and the like snapped back into place'.

The more I went to her the more aware I became of what was happening and in my trancelike state I was able to imagine what was happening inside of me.

Once I remember seeing what looked like a limp and flattened tubular pipe being inflated with a red beam of light which flowed along the tube seemingly revitalizing its life and restoring it to its proper shape.

This was very interesting; David was sharing with me the ability to see his meridian lines. This heightened vision during healing quite often happens with people who are psychic, like the young woman who could see colours. David is not in fact psychic, but very powerful healing seems to enable some people to experience psychic vision, which is lovely, in the same way that people's colour perception is often enhanced. Seeing colours as brighter after healing is a quite common experience. When people receive a powerful injection of life force this expands the mind energy outwards further than usual, enabling them to link up to the next dimension just enough to experience colours as they are experienced in that dimension.

John was another total sceptic who came to me with a very physical problem. An athletic nice-looking man in his thirties, he has his own publishing business and is extremely astute. We met at a party given by a mutual friend who told the guests before I arrived that I was a healer, clairvoyant and medium; most of them were keen to meet me, but John was quite uninterested.

However, when I arrived I went over to him and said: 'I don't know why, but I have to come and introduce myself to you.' We had an instant rapport, and for a while chatted away quite happily. When I told him I was a healer he said: 'I don't believe in all that.' I just laughed and said: 'I heal the non-believers as well!'

While we were talking I understood why I'd felt impelled to talk to him; somebody called Jack began pestering me to communicate with him urgently, so I asked if he would mind letting him come through. Still disbelieving, John said he had no objection. The information came through quickly; Jack said that he had owned a motorbike and sidecar, mentioned several names and described a variety of buildings in south London. His urgency was because John's mother hadn't been well recently, and Jack and her other spirit friends wanted to help her. I told John that he must contact his mother; all this information was really for her.

A few days later, John phoned his mother and passed this on. She confirmed that she'd had an Uncle Jack with a motorbike and sidecar; the area he had described was his home, and the people he had named were relatives she had known when young. She also said that she hadn't been well, though she was now feeling much better.

The details of the survival evidence were unimportant in themselves, but the fact that they were accurate gave John some food for thought! About a year later we met again; I reminded him of our talk and asked if his mother had confirmed the information. When he told me she had, I pulled his leg and said that I preferred more instant confirmation! I was also able to tell him that the survival evidence had been given as a catalyst to bring him closer to his mother, with whom he had not been on very good terms.

By now, John's attitude had totally changed from indifference to great interest. He was even more surprised when I asked him what had happened to his right calf muscle, which I could tell had atrophied. I had to laugh at John's startled expression as he said: 'How the hell can you see through my trousers?'

He told me that a few years earlier he had broken both legs in several places while playing football. Owing to complications he had spent nearly twelve months in plaster; his right leg had wasted, and he had spent many months trying to build up the muscles in order to run without a limp. More recently, he had completed an intense two-week course of physiotherapy at Headley Court Hospital which had been very successful; he had followed this up with regular training at a gymnasium. However, he still had a problem. Whenever he stopped training the calf muscle visibly shrank.

I felt sure I could help him, and got him to lie on my healing-couch. Here is John's account of what happened next:

Betty held my ankle in one hand and placed her other hand over the now healed break. She sat quietly and calmly and I was completely relaxed. After a few minutes she asked if I felt anything and I explained that from the knee downwards my leg was cold.

During the healing, I was given more survival evidence, but this time the names and information meant something to me and I was able to confirm that everything passed on to me was correct.

When I left that first healing session, which lasted an hour, I felt physically and mentally stimulated and was looking forward to seeing Betty again in a week's time. In the back of my mind I still had a doubt that Betty could stop my muscle from shrinking, but what could I lose! There was no way that I could be fooled, either my muscle would stop shrinking or not. A measuring tape would provide the evidence. But this time I had stopped training.

When Betty started healing my leg, the right calf muscle was smaller than my left. After only two sessions my right calf muscle was bigger than my left! When I told Betty on arrival for my third healing, she laughed and said it would settle down; both muscles would soon be the same size and I would not have any more problems with wasting. She was quite correct and I am pleased to say that, in the years that have followed, the calf muscle remains strong and despite having done no training the size has been constant.

John and I have been good friends ever since, and have spent many enjoyable hours discussing the philosophy of

life, death, religion and healing. He has since recommended me to many of his friends. One had an ear
problem and had been put on a waiting-list to see a
consultant; rather than wait six months, she came to see
me and her hearing was restored.

I have been able to restore hearing many times. In the
majority of these cases, I have seen clairvoyantly that the
deafness was apparently caused by a small amount of
calcium building up and spreading from a bone in the
inner ear (usually as the after-effect of a virus), which
healing energy can easily disperse. I've also had a lot of
success with Menière's disease.

Another friend of John's was Len, who came while he
was here on a visit from Australia. He had been blind
in one eye for twenty years and now, after a series of
haemorrhages behind the other eye, he had no sight at all.
His wife had to lead him by the hand everywhere. He had
seen consultants at three major eye hospitals, all of whom
had told him that he had no hope of ever regaining his
sight.

After the first healing, John's father took him to London.
When they arrived at Paddington Station, Len announced:
'I can see the lights!' From that moment on his sight
began steadily to return. When he returned to Australia I
continued giving him absent healing with my 'laser beam'
technique. A year later, on his next visit to England, he
came to see me. He walked in by himself, looked at me
and said: 'You look exactly how I thought you would!' It
was a very emotional reunion.

Len can now write his own letters, decorate and play
golf – with help, because his long-distance sight is not
marvellous. But he can see!

Although it's an area that I love, not many blind people
have come to me for healing; I would like to do more of
it. I would certainly never claim to be able to heal *all* cases
of blindness, but over the years I have brought sight back
to about ten people. Of one of them I have particularly
vivid memories.

Peter's blindness had been caused by a disease that strikes young men, and he had been told it was incurable. He came for about ten healings, and by the seventh we were both getting a bit despondent as there seemed to be no change. But after the eighth healing he suddenly said: 'Betty, I can see a candle, flickering, as though being blown by the wind.' I couldn't be sure what it meant; he was seeing it with his inner vision, and we were both delving in the dark. But I said: 'Peter, I think candlelight means hope!'

After that the candle never left him; he could see it all the time. His tenth session was his last with me as he had to move away; I suggested that he go to George Chapman, a healer who specializes in eye problems. He wrote to Mr Chapman, but before he could visit him he went on holiday to Scotland. On his first morning there he woke up with his sight completely restored!

Peter didn't know whether George Chapman had actually received his letter; but, as I told him, so long as he was cured, what did it matter? Possibly writing the letter had linked him in with Mr Chapman's healing energies, just as people who think of me receive help whether I am aware of it or not. I believe now that the vision of the candle was sent to him as a message to say: 'Hang in there, there is hope!'

There are still far too many cases which are classed as incurable because the doctors are baffled. The reason is usually that negative energy congestion is pressing on a vital spot and undermining the working of a major organ or other part of the body. Despite the incredible feats of medical science, nothing has yet been devised medically that can detect the most basic requirement of all existence: life-force energy. And so the real cause of countless complaints goes unrecognized and untreated.

Fred, for instance, whom I introduced in the last chapter, had had a total of eighty-nine hospital tests in an effort to trace the cause of his problem!

Shortly after the episode of the hob-nailed boots, Shirley contacted me to ask me to give Fred some healing. He had been suffering from what seemed to be a virus infection, which had steadily grown worse over the previous year. He had pains in his legs and hands, and great difficulty in breathing, and had eventually collapsed with a high fever.

He was tested for all kinds of infection from Lassa fever and glandular fever to all known viruses at the Hospital for Tropical Diseases. All the tests proved negative, and Fred was eventually discharged: the doctors could not identify anything to treat!

He came to see me in October 1978, a slim, quiet, rather shy man and a little sceptical of healing. I couldn't identify the virus, either, but of course I was able to work on his energy system, and I knew I could get him better. At that point his energy counterpart seemed drawn totally inwards, into an almost solid mass, rather than having the vibrating appearance to be seen around a healthy person. He came weekly until shortly before Christmas, for five sessions in all. Within two weeks he was feeling noticeably better, and by the end he was completely cured, with his energy system back to normal. Afterwards he wrote: 'I can now honestly say that I feel better than I have done for several years – my breathing is normal, I am sleeping well and most of all, I am now leading a healthy and energetic life once more. As I am still in my early 40s, this is most important.'

Both Shirley and Fred received a lot of healing and clairvoyance from me. During one of Fred's healing sessions he told me he had a cancerous wart on his head which was going to be surgically removed. When I gave him healing, I knew that the operation wouldn't be necessary, and told him so. Two weeks later the growth had disappeared.

When Fred next visited his doctor he told him what had happened. The doctor examined him and confirmed that the growth had gone. This doctor was more open-minded than some; he had heard similar stories before, he said, and wasn't altogether surprised.

There are some diseases which healing cannot always help, especially when the condition has advanced too far to reverse it; occasionally, too, I come across a few people who for some reason just don't respond to healing. These days, however, I am specializing in so-called incurable cases, and sometimes the results are beyond my expectations! Currently, for instance, I have been getting good results with a man with motor neurone disease.

From my point of view, it appears that with this crippling disease the blood-supply to the nerves going through the muscles has been cut off. As I've mentioned, healing energy works very well with circulatory problems. This particular man's leg was completely bloodless when he first came, and as cold as a marble slab; during the first healing he experienced the energy like a series of electric shocks. When he returned home his big toe became red and swollen, as the blood-supply returned. On his second visit, he was already walking about the room with no support, for the first time for months, and is overjoyed as the use of his muscles returns.

I would never claim, however, to be able to cure motor neurone disease. Sometimes it takes over the system very rapidly, and once it is advanced, sadly, I can do nothing about it. But anyone with a disease like this, including multiple sclerosis or muscular dystrophy, could gain an awful lot of benefit if their muscles were strengthened by healing energy.

Another disease the doctors find hard to treat, and with which I have had quite a lot of success, is rheumatoid arthritis, whose effects can be agonizing. Shirley's mother, for instance, had suffered from it for many years and was in constant pain; she couldn't even bear to be touched. As is common with this disease, her bones had been affected. Her legs had become misshapen, and her arms would no longer straighten, so that her coat-sleeves had to be shortened. It was becoming increasingly difficult for her to hold a cup of tea without dropping it.

Shirley brought her to see me in December 1979, and she came regularly at monthly intervals for four years; since she had to travel quite a distance she couldn't come more often. It was necessary to keep the healing going because of her age; older people do need more healing than the young, especially if the physical body has deteriorated in other ways, as hers had.

Even so, as the months went by a wonderful improvement took place; her legs began to straighten out, the inflammation left her hands and she became virtually pain-free for the first time for twenty years. Because I had to move, she was unable to visit me after those four years and, as happens in old people, the arthritis took over again. But at least before she died she had some pain-free and enjoyable years which she would not otherwise have had.

In younger people the healing is generally total and they do not need years of treatment. One young woman of twenty-eight had been unable to walk for years because both her hips were completely frozen by arthritis. She had had an operation to release one hip but complained when she came to see me: 'I can't move my other leg, although the doctors say with exercise I should be able to.'

When I looked at her I felt that the first operation had been unnecessary: it was clear to me that she was locked at the *pelvis* and not at the hips. So I worked on her pelvic joint, which was packed with calcium deposits, and little by little got the leg moving – each time with the usual bangs, cracks and explosions! I asked her to let me know if it hurt, but she assured me that it didn't. After these explosions there would be a satisfying increase in the mobility of her leg. In the end, though she still limped on the side that had been operated on, the untouched leg and hip were completely cured.

Sometimes surgery is essential, but even then healing can help speed up recovery. In 1979, Shirley was coming to see me regularly for clairvoyance, and usually had healing as well. I knew that she had some health problems, which she also knew about, and at one session I told her that she would have to take an enforced rest. Shortly afterwards she was admitted to hospital for an emergency hysterectomy. Afterwards the doctor telephoned Fred to say that if she hadn't had the operation then she would only have lived a month, as her bladder had deteriorated and was causing extensive complications. Shirley would need six months' rest to recover completely.

I gave her absent healing while she was in hospital, and when she came out she visited me for contact healing. After two weeks she went for a hospital check-up: the surgeon told her he had never seen such a rapid recovery; she was doing far better than some patients who had had less serious operations. She was completely better within a month: orthodox surgery and healing combined had produced the perfect cure.

Another young woman, Leah, went ahead with an operation which turned out not to be necessary. Leah is a very attractive and lively young businesswoman, who had previously been to see me for her severe tension in the summer of 1980, and recovered beautifully. (This story is told in the next chapter.) A couple of years later she was advised by a leading gynaecologist to have an immediate operation for the removal of a cyst. This was just before Christmas and, although it was urgent, she persuaded the surgeon to postpone it until the New Year.

In the meantime, she came to see me and asked my advice. I gave her some healing straight away, during which a voice told me: 'They won't find anything!' So, at the end of the session, I said: 'There, they won't find a thing!' Leah stared at me incredulously, and reminded me that she'd been examined by two very capable professionals. This is Leah's account of what happened next:

The day of the operation arrived and I had long since dismissed Betty's claim. I confess here and now, with a canyon full of grovelling apologies, that I did not believe her.

I was wheeled down to the hospital theatre and lost my senses until a few hours later when I saw my surgeon standing over me in the recovery room. He asked how I felt and I struggled to regain my thoughts and focus. I felt droopy, but not in the least sore or pained. I told him so.

'That's not surprising,' he said. 'It's quite extraordinary, but we couldn't find anything there.'

Over the years a number of people have come to me for help with cancer of various kinds, and sometimes healing can bring about a cure. I have had some remarkable successes with breast cancer, especially when the women concerned have come to me early. Some fifty in all have come to me with lumps in the breast; about thirty-five had already been diagnosed as having cancer, while the others were too scared to have medical tests. In about half of them the lumps have simply disappeared beneath my hands in one session. Sue's problems were bigger than this, however.

Sue is a management consultant, a slim dark lady in her forties whose deceptively quiet manner conceals a lot of determination. She had already survived two encounters with cancer, in her twenties and again in her thirties, despite the appalling physical and mental side-effects of radiation and chemotherapy, and despite being sent home at one point to write her will! When it struck a third time she refused further medical treatment and decided to conquer the disease by willpower alone. She was helped by a new man-friend who provided plenty of emotional support; she acquired a new job and a new home, and believed she was definitely 'on the up'.

'It's extraordinary', writes Sue, 'how certain scenes are

transfixed in your memory, like still pictures suddenly held in a motion film.'

In my case I had just reached the landing in my new home and was turning back to my guest, still with my hand on the banister, when he said, 'Sue, I think you ought to see Betty. She's a wonderful healer and a great friend of mine.'

The implication was instantly obvious. I wasn't winning the battle with the cancer I thought I had already defeated. For once in my chequered career I had everything going for me, and I honestly thought I had already beaten the 'big C' by mind over matter. The magic of that evening and my pride in my new home were destroyed in that instant. I remember arguing that I was OK, marvellous; a bit tired perhaps but fit as a fiddle, and I didn't need any mumbo-jumbo. I also remember being bullied by everybody there into making an appointment with Betty on the basis that it couldn't do any harm anyhow.

Sue never kept her first appointment; by accident or by design she got lost *en route*. She phoned to apologize, and agreed to come back bringing her man-friend for moral support. (I'm always quite happy for people to bring their partners or friends along with them.) Both were sceptical when they arrived, Sue because she still refused to accept that she wasn't well, and Dennis because he thought healers were a 'highly dubious mixture of charlatans, spiritual pontificators and well-meaning, but powerless, do-gooders!' Sue writes:

I was the first to succumb. Betty was large, lovely, overflowing with warmth and compassion and a compulsive giggler. I loved and trusted her on sight.

Dennis was knocked out when she politely enquired how successful the operation on his right Achilles tendon had been. She could only have known about that clairvoyantly.

Sue seemed very clear about what was wrong with her, and told me she wasn't going to go through any more chemotherapy or radiation treatment. I am always very careful what I say when giving people a clairvoyant diagnosis, but from what she told me I assumed that her medical advisers had put her fully in the picture. I told her that the most serious problems, and the most difficult to heal, were the breakdown of the intestinal lining of her lower bowel and the deterioration of the walls of her veins and arteries. I could also see that she had a blood problem: there were clearly too many white cells, indicating a form of leukaemia.

When I told Sue this, she said: 'I beg your pardon?'

'Haven't they told you?' I asked.

'No, they bloody well haven't!' said Sue. I felt bad about this, and hastened to assure her that healing is very good for blood and circulation problems. By the end of the healing session Sue was very relaxed, and,

. . . profoundly relieved someone was taking a personal interest in me, knew exactly what was wrong and offered a reasonable but not totally optimistic prognosis. A few days later, before my next treatment, I phoned the GP who had seen me through my most difficult days before I had moved south.

'Why didn't you tell me the damn thing was destroying my whole blood and circulatory system?' I demanded.

'Who the hell was stupid enough to tell you that?' was his reply. 'You've got enough problems coping with the cancer you do know about, without some stupid so-and-so telling you that you are riddled with additional problems which nobody can do anything about.'

It wasn't a typical GP's reply, but then he wasn't a typical GP. . . When I explained about Betty, his only reaction was positive. He firmly believed that cancer was caused by emotional and physical trauma or strain triggering off a natural or genetic propensity in the cell structure. He knew my case history. He'd also seen many people who should have recovered from cancer just lie down and die, and equally others who'd recovered against all the medical odds. His advice was, 'If you believe it will help you, go ahead,' and I did.

The fact that I had given her a correct diagnosis, even if it was a shock to her, was very convincing to Sue. She came to see me regularly for healing after that; she never once doubted that she would be cured, even though it was some time before I was sure myself. Quite early on she was given a spiritual operation, during which the smell of ether made her feel choked and nauseous. The vividness of this experience, and the realization that there was no way that I could have manufactured it myself, increased her faith in healing.

Although she had been far from positive at her first visit, once she began to feel well again and realized that healing could really help her, her own positive attitude carried her through. At a medical examination some five months later, she told the doctor absolutely truthfully that she couldn't remember when she had felt so well. He gave her a clean bill of health; all the tests failed to find any trace of cancer or any abnormality in her blood. 'As an additional bonus,' says Sue, 'my bowels were regular for the first time since childhood!'

That was five years ago. In the interim Sue has developed spondulitis and arthritis, as the aftermath of a serious accident which prompted one company doctor to turn her down for a job on the basis that she'd be in a wheelchair within three years. She isn't! She came back to see me and is perfectly fit again. She writes: 'In the past few months I have stripped wallpaper and plaster, painted ceilings, humped carpets etc. with only the usual aches and pains. . . Betty has stopped a progressively degenerative disease progressing.'

Not surprisingly, Sue is still anxious about a possible recurrence of cancer. About four years after she recovered, she started bleeding heavily from the rectum and immediately panicked. She was in Europe at the time, and her man-friend's instant reaction was to phone me for help rather than to call a local doctor. I told her: 'Don't worry, it's not serious, but it does need treatment. Go to the doctor.' She did, and found that it was simply a non-malignant polyp which was easily removed. She writes:

> It's tempting to eulogize someone who has given you the gift of health and strength and an unexpected lease and quality of life; to wax emotional and to try and find reasons and explanations for it all. The simple fact is that Betty's particular magic cured me when the medical profession had given up. Equally I know that she will help me through any future illness, even if that help means making my inevitable death one day a dignified and relatively painless exit.

Letters like this are proof of the seemingly impossible being achieved in the gentlest manner, and that the energies around us can be harnessed and used. Sue speaks of 'magic'; I would say that a healer is an alchemist who transmutes life force into a mixture of elements which alter the complex physical make-up of the body, bringing about changes which are far beyond current scientific expectations.

The attitude of Sue's doctor must have helped her a lot. So many people still lack the courage to tell their doctors when they benefit from healing; this is one reason why healing has so long remained an undercover operation. Fortunately, the tide is turning pretty rapidly and nearly all the people who visit me now speak openly about the help they receive. To their doctors' credit they very rarely receive a negative response.

It has not so far been possible for me to demonstrate the potential of healing to an audience of English doctors, but in 1982 I was invited to participate in a medical seminar on healing in Segovia in Spain. Because it has only recently been possible to practise healing openly in Spain, Spanish doctors are much more fascinated by the whole subject than most English doctors. The English have been aware of the existence of healing for so many years that they tend to shrug it off without really investigating it. By contrast, at the end of the Segovia seminar all the doctors I spoke to said in heartfelt tones that they were sorry that something so wonderful had been kept from them! As a group, they were the friendliest members of the medical profession I have ever met.

I travelled there with Barry Stonehill, a friend who has travelled the world testing all kinds of alternative healing methods. On the way we stopped in Madrid, where Barry invited me to meet a friend, an elderly man whom he described as an 'old boulevardier'. Since he was always on the move, Barry used to drop in on friends abroad at rather short notice!

When we arrived at this man's house, we were both shocked to discover that he was blind. He was in his seventies, and had developed cataracts in both eyes which were not yet 'ripe' to be operated on. Barry at once announced that I was a healer and asked if he would like some healing; the old gentleman thought we were joking, and just laughed. The joke, as Barry said afterwards, was on him.

We were going out to eat, and didn't have much time.

I wasn't sure that I could help the man, because his eyes were extremely cloudy, so I said I would give him fifteen minutes' healing, and boost this with absent healing later. After the fifteen minutes were up the 'boulevardier' got up, walked out on to the terrace and exclaimed: 'My God, I can see the flowers!' That seemed miraculous even to me, and I said: '*Can* you?' The old gentleman was quite overcome; he kept saying: 'I don't believe it. I can see you and I can see the flowers!'

Some of the most fantastic healings, I find, occur when I don't feel I've really done anything.

An hour later the 'boulevardier' took us out to a restaurant, guiding us all the way there. He was anxious to know whether his sight would last. I couldn't be sure, because I had the impression that he didn't take very good care of himself, and hardened arteries contribute to the formation of cataract; however, when Barry rang him a month or so later his sight was still fine.

The seminar itself lasted five days, and I worked about twelve hours a day. The healers and therapists were allocated to small groups for most of the time, and we got together at the end for a summing-up. In my group, as well as healing I was giving clairvoyance, survival evidence, clairvoyant diagnosis and hypnotherapy.

There were about five hundred delegates, practically all in the medical profession, some of whom had brought patients to be 'guinea pigs'. There were a few sceptics among them, but healings took place that even they simply could not discount. For me, the outstanding memory is the impact we had on one particular doctor.

One of the people I was asked to take a look at was a man of perhaps thirty, who had come with his medical practitioner; he had been unable to walk unaided for two years, and despite numerous investigations nobody had been able to find out why. I could immediately see clairvoyantly that the artery in his groin was kinked, probably owing to a thinning of the artery wall, and this was cutting off the blood-supply to his leg. I gave him healing in the form of a psychic operation which straightened out the artery, and finished the session with hypnotherapy to help him stop chain-smoking, which could have been contributing to his circulation problems.

When we'd finished, the man got up saying he felt very dizzy. He went outside, walking perfectly normally – and immediately lit up a cigarette! You can't win them all!

On our return journey to Madrid, Barry and I stopped off at a bar on the highway for a snack. As we walked into the bar we were approached by this man and his doctor, who were also there. They were delighted. The doctor told us that he had thoroughly examined his patient and that he had been completely cured. Two years later I heard that he was still fine.

In years to come, such cures will be commonplace, in much the same way that past discoveries like electricity, broadcasting and space travel have become part of our everyday life; and, as our knowledge has progressed, our minds have had to open up to accept the evidence.

It is still rare for a doctor to seek healing; perhaps half a dozen have come to me in my thirteen years as a healer. However, even doctors are sometimes told to 'learn to live with it', and pushed to seek alternatives.

I'd like to tell you Anton's story in some detail, because as a doctor with a totally scientific training he had been taught to 'question science and to question all phenomena from a scientific point of view', and was unable to believe in anything without scientific evidence to back it up.

Anton had worked in the National Health Service for twenty years as a clinical biochemist and was also a Doctor of Philosophy. In 1976 his younger daughter had started doing gymnastics; since she was clearly gifted Anton and his wife decided to help her by qualifying as club coaches, as defined by the British Amateur Gymnastics Association. They worked hard and, while the child's skills improved, so did her parents' coaching abilities. Anton went on to teach gymnastics at national level, which meant supporting children in advanced moves – and that was how he came to damage his left elbow.

He went to see an orthopaedic surgeon at his hospital, who diagnosed tennis elbow and prescribed a steroid injection together with physiotherapy three times a week for three weeks. After three weeks, however, the arm was no better. The surgeon advised a further steroid injection and a further course of physiotherapy. 'Needless to say,' writes Anton, 'my arm did not recover.'

The surgeon then suggested an operation consisting of stripping the muscle from the attachment to the bone in the elbow. This would lessen the pain and allow the irritated torn attachment to heal itself, so Anton agreed. It was a number of weeks before the pain subsided and Anton had enough strength to use his arm normally, aided by further physiotherapy and strengthening exercises. Then, feeling that his body was healed, he went back to coaching his daughter. As he realized later, this was a mistake.

As a doctor, he found it 'interesting' that, although he had no further pain in his elbow, his shoulder now became painful and grew worse as he continued coaching. He returned down the 'well-trodden path to the orthopaedic surgeon', who recommended an injection in the shoulder, followed by further physiotherapy.

Some five weeks later the shoulder was still painful. Yet another injection was followed by five more weeks of pain, by which time Anton was practically immobile and had given up coaching. There was a further injection, and a further five weeks of pain with still no improvement.

At this point, Anton couldn't lift his left arm even to put a jacket on; his wife had to help him dress. By now he had received the maximum amount of steroid deemed safe, and his colleague told him nothing further could be done medically: Anton must come to terms with the fact that he was disabled.

During this time he had become a consultant clinical biochemist and had been working closely with a publisher, my friend John, who suggested he should consider seeing a healer. Like many scientists, Anton recognized the existence of healing, but since he couldn't understand it scientifically it was to be several months before he was prepared to try it. One day, however, John rang me up while Anton was visiting him. He told me 'a doctor friend' was having problems with his elbow but was very sceptical and could not be persuaded to visit me personally. I said: 'I think you'll find your friend's problem is with his shoulder.'

John checked this out, and of course Anton confirmed that indeed the problem was now in his shoulder. Perhaps that helped him to overcome his reluctance to visit me, though even after making an appointment he was 'filled with trepidation'; his idea of a healer was of 'someone who would go into a trance, make some strange noises and really become quite abnormal'. However, like others before him, he felt he had nothing to lose, and kept his appointment.

Here is Anton's account of what actually happened.

When I met Betty, I was surprised to find that she was a very ordinary person, very lively and very friendly. Quite different to what I was expecting. She explained what she was going to do and that I would probably need to see her five or six times. She then put her hands on my shoulder and closed her eyes. Her hands became very warm and I felt extremely comfortable.

Betty then explained that she was receiving messages. There was no doubt in my mind that she was indeed receiving information from my grandparents who had died a number of years previously. The interesting thing was that her description of my grandmother, an unusual person, was extremely accurate. There was no way she had got any of this information from me. I could not explain it but there was no doubt that she was learning about me when I was a child.

I had to accept it for what it was. Very difficult if all your life you have been testing hypotheses and receiving scientific answers. The interesting thing was the message my grandmother had given Betty – 'I must believe.'

I must admit, when I left Betty I was beginning to believe.

Although it took him over an hour to drive home, Anton's left shoulder was still hot when he arrived; he asked his wife to feel it, and she could feel the heat, too.

After Anton had visited me once a week for four weeks the pain had gone completely and he had total movement in his left arm. Being a scientist, however, he still felt that his recovery could be a coincidence. He tested it out by coaching gymnastics again, including teaching the somersault that had caused the problem in the first place. I had actually told him to stop coaching; the muscles and tendons had been damaged by the operation, and his arm really wasn't strong enough to resume that kind of activity. However, although he was 'beginning to believe', he had to prove to himself that the healing had in fact taken place.

About a year later, in 1982, his shoulder not surprisingly became extremely painful again. He rang me for another appointment: as soon as he arrived I knew at once that he had been coaching gymnastics again. His pain vanished after one session, but his tendons had been damaged by the operation, and I knew he would be in trouble again if he continued his activities. I told him that he must stop, if he wanted to remain pain-free.

Anton was satisfied by now with his experiment on himself, that healing worked. 'There was no doubt in my mind, that healing had removed the pain. Healing had healed my shoulder,' he writes. Now that he was completely convinced, he decided that he ought to know more about healing, and came to see me specifically to talk about it. He was worried about the occasions during his work in the National Health Service when the side-effects of drugs given to patients were worse than their original illness. Healing struck him as a 'far nicer, non-invasive technique'. I knew that like many doctors he had healing gifts himself, and told him so. Writes Anton:

By now I was no longer surprised by what Betty had to say. Her predictions generally came true. She explained to me that I would be leaving the Health Service. At the time I was extremely happy and could see no reason for leaving. As it transpired, I started to help Betty and after a number of months I began to see people by myself at home to help them with healing. Also, as Betty had predicted, I had become disenchanted with the National Health Service and decided to leave. I set up a partnership with my publisher friend and it is becoming quite successful.

Anton came and joined in my healing sessions, which I found very interesting as he was able to describe people's problems from the medical point of view. Within three months he was receiving clairvoyant diagnosis, not 'seeing' in the way that I do, or receiving spirit messages, but through an inner knowing.

This inner knowing – which I am sure many doctors possess – coupled with his medical knowledge, enabled him to tell people exactly what was wrong, and his healing became daily more effective. Although he only heals part-time as he has a family to support, he has the potential to work successfully as a full-time healer. He also has those essential qualities, compassion and love for his fellow-men.

Long ago when doctors had more time they used to sit

at the bedside and hold their patient's hands and say: 'You will feel better tomorrow.' These doctors were natural healers; they didn't use many drugs, because they weren't available. By holding the patient's hands a healing energy flowed from the doctor and the healing process had begun. I have come across several doctors who have been natural healers without knowing it; they are not only successful medical men; they also have an abundance of love and compassion.

No one can work really effectively as a healer without possessing compassion for every living thing; to heal, compassion must be present in the very essence of your being.

SIX

Helping the Healing Process

🦋

My once sceptical friend John has written the following:

Betty has much to offer in teaching new ways of keeping healthy and healing ourselves. She has taught me techniques that I have applied with minimum practice and have found to be a great help in controlling stress and my reactions to the difficulties which we all inevitably suffer throughout life.

We are our own beings and can learn to control our own mind energies. Good health is our own responsibility rather than somebody else's. How we react to life's problems is really in our own hands. It has always been my opinion that there is more to this life than meets the eye and Betty has proved to me that this is true. I am a better person both physically and mentally through the experience and plan to continue learning.

A good deal is written these days about self-responsibility for health. Sometimes I think that this is overdone; it doesn't help people who are already ill to be made to feel guilty about it. However, there is no doubt that the main causes of blockages in the energy system are stress, negativity, and abuse of the physical body with bad diet, alcohol, smoking and drugs, medical and otherwise. So, although many ailments can be cured with healing, to get really well again it is often necessary for people to make changes in their lifestyle and attitudes. The healing process is not a passive one, and many of those who have come to me have made tremendous efforts to help themselves.

At the same time, 'self-responsibility' doesn't mean that you have to struggle along on your own; we are all here to help and co-operate with one another. Seeking and accepting the help of a healer or other therapist is a part of helping oneself. Very often, indeed, people need an outsider to show them why they have become ill: it's amazing how difficult it is to see things for oneself, or to realize what bad habits one has got into. I know, because for years I was addicted to sugar without realizing it, although my children could see it!

It is only after becoming sick that many people realize what health really means. Using clairvoyance, I can always see what changes may be needed but, while I can advise, it's up to the person concerned to take that advice and heed early warnings while a cure can still be brought about. I still use my knowledge of vitamin and mineral therapy, but these days I don't recommend anything until the patient has already had one or two healing sessions at regular weekly intervals to boost his energy. Once his energy has been built up it can be maintained with the right nutrition and mental attitudes.

The very first essential for good health is a positive attitude to life; negativity and stress are at the root of most problems, including self-destructive habits. No doubt from time to time everyone has been told to 'think positive', and it isn't always easy. As I can actually *see* what happens when they do, I can explain just why it is so helpful; for many people this has opened a hitherto closed door. At the end of their first session I tell new patients something about mind energy, so that they can practise being positive before their next visit. When they next come I will be able to see from the state of their mind energy whether they have been working at it, and this thought encourages them to keep going!

I also encourage them by teaching them relaxation techniques and mind-expanding exercises, some of which are included in the last section of this book. Healing can eliminate negative energy, but the regular practice of positive thought is needed to prevent a renewed build-up of adverse energies. Unless negativity can be reversed there is always a risk of falling ill again. In the end we have to cure ourselves with positivity.

Sue, whom I told you about in the last chapter, felt very low when she first came to see me, but she was a real fighter. I am certain that her recovery was due to the combination of healing and her positive attitude. For people who are negative, I always suggest putting a time-limit on negative thoughts and then, when the time is up, cutting them off. Being miserly with negative time can change your whole life!

It would be asking too much to expect ill people to arrive on my doorstep radiating positivity, and indeed most of them don't! But an open mind and a receptive attitude make a good start; and, if there is also a good rapport with the healer, healing of both mind and body can take place remarkably quickly. Leah, too, was feeling very low when she came to see me in 1980 suffering from extreme tension, owing to difficulties relating to her work, boyfriend, daughter and parents! In addition, she was yet another person who came 'with considerable trepidation', expecting 'a wrinkled lady with headscarf, hooped ear-rings and a regular stand at Blackpool Pier!' Writes Leah:

> When the door opened I saw . . . a smiling face, with 'welcome' written from one cheek to the next. Her eyes gazed at me like two lasers and I knew in that instant that any airs or pretences that I had acquired in my life had to be left on the doormat. She could see straight into my soul; yet somehow I felt at ease.

When Leah had hopped on to my healing-couch, a number of people immediately began to communicate with her. Leah says:

I was amazed not only by the accuracy of the survival evidence but also by my own attitude. I simply was not afraid. I recall quite clearly Betty describing my maternal grandmother. This was followed by a request for me to be more patient with my mother. At that time, because of all the stress, I had been quite cantankerous, and I instantly felt guilty, recalling at least half a dozen instances of gross misconduct and insubordination on my part!

A great deal more evidence poured forth, much of which really startled Leah. She was able to identify most of the people who communicated, in particular a young cousin who had died in a car crash some eight years before; any pieces of information she didn't understand were confirmed later when she checked them with members of her family.

While all this was going on, Leah was allowing herself to be completely receptive to the healing I was giving her. She simply soaked it up! When she left, she had to sit for a moment in her car, to contemplate her new-found composure.

All the tension had gone, and I felt a far greater lucidity of thought than I'd ever experienced. Betty did not tell me what to do; it was unnecessary. I knew it purely by instinct. I knew the job had to go and so did the troublesome boyfriend. I knew which situations in my family called for greater compassion and which for increased rigidity. I began to arrange my attitudes accordingly and the effects were dramatic.

The effects certainly were dramatic; the turn-round in Leah's attitudes and her resolution to straighten out her life opened the way for much more happiness to come in. I had also given her clairvoyance: I could see that she would travel; I could see her photograph in magazines, and I could also see her linked romantically with an ambassador! Although her father was a diplomat, she felt the last prediction was laughable, especially when I told her he would be short, balding and portly, the antithesis of the men she was usually attracted to.

In fact all these predictions turned out to be absolutely correct. Leah's totally positive response to that one healing session enabled her to continue developing in both positivity and spiritual awareness. In this respect healing can be like sowing a seed which grows despite yourself. Leah went on to do jobs that she would never have thought she would cope with. And eventually she did meet a man who exactly fitted my description. She found her 'knees jellifying at the sound of his voice, which seemed to emanate from the soil, it was so deep and resonant. I simply did not see his face. . . What I saw came from within, and he had an enormous reservoir of love in his heart.' It wasn't until some time after this meeting that Leah discovered that he was an ambassador!

Unfortunately, over the last twenty years a very common medical answer to depression and anxiety has been to prescribe tranquillizers, which block the energy system further and can actually prevent people from sorting out the problems that are causing the stress.

Now that it's been discovered that tranquillizers are addictive, many doctors are much more cautious about doling them out and encourage patients to find other ways of relaxing. A lot of suffering could be avoided if people under stress would seek the help of a healer, and back this up by practising relaxation and positive thinking at home. Take Doris, for example, the sister of Margery, whom I told you about in the last chapter.

When Margery's migraines were cured so dramatically, Doris asked to come and see me, too. She had suffered untold miseries because of a wrong medical diagnosis. In fact, just like Margery, she had painful arthritis in the back of her neck, accompanied by migraines and insomnia, but she had received quite different treatment from her sister's. Her doctor never looked at her spine; he decided that the problem was 'nerves' and prescribed accordingly.

The first pills she was given had no effect on her migraines and insomnia; in fact they added to her problems by creating nervous side-effects. She felt permanently dizzy and light-headed, which made her afraid of traffic and terrified of going out. The doctor then prescribed Valium; this quietened the side-effects of the first pills, but the migraines and insomnia continued. By the time she came to see me she had been taking Valium for seven years and, like so many other unfortunate people, was totally addicted to it, although it made her feel like a zombie.

All chemical drugs have the effect of pushing the energy counterpart out of place, and the mind energy can be pushed upwards so that the person is slightly out of his body! A similar effect happens naturally when you are asleep, but going around like this during the day makes people feel very peculiar. Many of them say they feel as if their feet are not fully on the ground; in energy terms, they aren't, since the energy has been drawn up and away from the feet.

When Doris arrived, I saw at once that the colour in her aura was the yellow that indicated arthritis, not the green of a nervous problem at all. In addition, the mind energy around the top of her head was only a thin line, instead of a vibrant cloud of energy; I have seen this same phenomenon in other people with problems of addiction; it may have something to do with the suppression of electrical currents.

When Doris lay down, I could see yellow energy congested all around her neck, while dark areas of negative energy throughout her body indicated that some major areas were under stress. As I gave her healing I said: 'Doris, you've got the same problem as Margery!' Just as with her sister, calcium was pressing on a vital nerve at the top of the spine.

I was also able to tell her that the problem had started in her energy counterpart at the time when she lost her mother, to whom she had been very close, and had manifested physically eighteen months later. Doris agreed that was exactly what had happened.

I laid my hands on her abdomen, which was very congested because of the drugs; when that had been partially cleared I went over the other congested areas. When I treated her neck, we could hear noises like splintering glass indicating that the calcium was breaking up; this happened on all of Doris's visits, until at last she was free from her arthritic prison.

Whenever I give healing, people go away afterwards glowing, and I can see a white light all round them. From Doris's first healing this brilliant white light came in, taking over all the dark patches and the yellow in her body. But I particularly remember her second session, because her energy counterpart was simply bathed in a beautiful pale blue, a very healing colour; it was as if an extra amount of healing energy was being given her. During this session she told me that she felt at peace for the first time in seven years.

When she realized how the Valium had been affecting her, Doris made up her mind to stop taking it there and then. I warned her to cut down her dosage by degrees to avoid withdrawal symptoms. However, Doris was determined, and threw her pills away overnight.

As a result, she did have extremely bad withdrawal symptoms for about two months, although regular healing made these attacks less ferocious than they would otherwise have been. One evening between appointments she phoned me to ask for help; she was due to meet some friends to celebrate her birthday but felt too ill to make the journey. I told her she would be able to go to the party; meanwhile she should just sit quietly until I phoned her back. I then gave her absent healing, visualizing her whole body surrounded in healing energies. I knew she would be all right.

When I rang her after twenty minutes she told me that after she sat down she lost all consciousness; when she was awakened by the telephone she thought she must have been asleep. But she felt so good that she knew she had been completely taken over by the healing energies. Later that evening she rang to say that she was at the hotel having a wonderful party!

Doris eventually stopped having withdrawal symptoms. She has not taken any drug since she first came to see me some six years ago. Doris was a case of severe addiction to tranquillizers and, although she didn't take my advice about dropping them slowly, her determination to take responsibility and fight the addiction was a vital factor in her recovery.

As a rule, I suggest to people who are on tranquillizers that they should only take one if they need it. Usually the healing energies smooth away their anxieties to such an extent that they need the pills less and less, and find themselves stopping gradually and naturally. Rather than giving up, they simply forget to take them.

Addiction comes in many forms. People who become hooked on medical drugs are usually innocent victims, but where cigarettes, alcohol and certain foods are concerned most of us have some choice, at least to start with. Smoking and food addictions I can usually help with hypnosis, provided the person really wants to give up. I think my attitude helps as well; as a former sugar addict, I can understand what it means to be hooked on something. When people realize I am not going to judge them, and know exactly what they are going through, the rapport helps with the healing.

Drink is a rather different problem; alcoholics really need more time and attention than I can give them, so I always suggest that they go to Alcoholics Anonymous, who do very good work and provide emotional support. If someone has already joined AA and stopped drinking, healing can of course boost his energy system and help him to feel better, but only the alcoholic can take the first steps.

Much the same is true of non-medical drug addicts. Again, most of them need more time and attention than an individual healer can give, though if healers were brought into withdrawal programmes they would certainly have a part to play. At one point, however, I found myself working with several young drug addicts who came to me through friends.

Drug addiction is a very worrying problem, not only for the obvious reasons, but also because drugs can attract very negative energies. One day I was visited by a boy in his teens, who came because of a knee injury. While I was healing him, I felt a very odd energy around him; I went cold and shivery, and had a feeling of repulsion. I asked him how he was feeling, and he said that while he was with me he felt safe, but there were times when he felt suicidal.

At that point I was given a clairvoyant message that he was on drugs. I checked this out with him, and he admitted that he was. I described the unpleasant energy I could sense around him, but didn't go into too much detail because I didn't want to frighten him. I explained to him that the drugs had affected his mind so that it had become alien to his true nature and had attracted unwanted negative energies. He wasn't surprised; in fact he was relieved, because that was what he had sensed himself. When he was alone he, too, could feel when these unpleasant energies were around, and felt cold and shivery and frightened. This is why many drug addicts feel paranoid: it's not just their imagination; they are actually attracting negativity.

We had a long talk, and I promised to see the young man once a week for the next few weeks. 'You can get rid of this feeling,' I told him, 'but it will mean a lot of hard work, and a change in your attitudes to life. I don't mean that you have to change your personality; simply that you will go back to being the nice person you were before you started taking drugs.'

It was to be several months before, together, we brought about a really positive change by strengthening his mind energy and boosting his depleted physical system. You have to feel better in yourself before you have the strength to use your mind to the full, especially when your strength has been sapped by drug-taking! We both went through many heartaches, but in the end he did change. He came off drugs, and the negative energy was eliminated. Once more he was in command of his own life, which is as it should be.

As this story shows, negativity can be dangerous. I have already mentioned Universal Law; it is a vital message that during my years as a medium has been repeated constantly. Whatever you do in thought, word and deed, pleasant or unpleasant, will return to you in the fullness of time. It may not necessarily come from the person you have loved or disliked, but you cannot escape from the effects of your own actions. We have no choice but to accept responsibility for what we do.

The Law of the Universe is unbending; there is no escaping it. I have studied people and situations for years, and in the end, no matter how long it may take, what one gives out comes back. Everything, whether it's anxiety, a piece of malicious gossip, or a loving and positive thought for someone else, takes the form of energy which in the end we will attract back to ourselves.

Universal Law cannot be changed. That is why this message cannot be ignored. Unless we accept this fact and change, even in small ways, our own destruction and eventually that of the earth will be irreversible.

This message has been preached by every major religion throughout time. It is obvious that many people today are becoming aware of it, and I believe the tide has started to turn, but progress must accelerate if we are going to make waves. There are hundreds of young people who have become vegetarian, and who are trying to prevent cruelty to animals. Ecologists everywhere are trying desperately to reverse the situation created by man's destruction of nature. More and more ordinary people are not only aware of the plight of others but are also taking action to help them.

We owe it to ourselves and to the people with whom we live to create a peaceful and loving environment. We also owe it to the whole world to share our peace and love and help those whose lives are beset with uncertainty and trauma. We can't all be saints, and I'm sure most of us don't want to be! But it will make life easier in the end not to give out any disagreeable vibrations; the energies we put out return to us in some form or other, and negative thinking will attract negative vibrations and even happenings.

Among the drug addicts who have sought my help, an understanding of Universal Law and the realization that ultimately we cannot escape from responsibility have been one of the main factors in their cure.

It is sad that young people turn to drugs for inspiration, when we can all contact our creativity in much happier ways. I have worked with a number of young musicians who have been addicted to all kinds of drug, believing that they enhanced their creativity. The danger is that drugs *may* give the young some kind of glimpse into another dimension, so they will ignore the fact that they are damaging their bodies and their brains. When they have healing, and experience phenomena such as colours coming through, they begin to understand that drugs are not the only way to touch into other worlds!

These musicians included Matt, who first visited me in 1983. He was twenty-one, a slim tense young man. He had dislocated his right shoulder several times during the previous eighteen months. Doctors and private specialists had told him that the only treatment available was a fairly serious operation which was not always successful. It would have left him with restricted movement and, as Matt puts it, 'I had been putting off making a decision because (*a*) I am a musician and (*b*) a coward.'

One of Matt's friends had already made an appointment to see me; Matt accompanied him on his first visit, and waited for him in the car. After the friend's healing session he told me about Matt, and I was able to see him there and then.

Matt was clearly feeling frightened as he walked in, not knowing what to expect, but he soon relaxed when he saw I wasn't a weirdo! As I laid my hands on his shoulder, I could tell there was some arthritis in there. He felt a dull heat flowing through his shoulder and arm, and we could hear the customary creaking and cracking.

Matt and his friend came together for their second visit; I had to tell them both that they were both blocked from drug and alcohol abuse. Neither of the boys really wanted to hear this and they didn't take much notice; drugs and drink were very much part of the music scene that they lived and worked in. But, as I explained to them, when someone has been for a long time on drugs – medical or otherwise – the energy system can become partially blocked, and in some parts closed down altogether. Then it desperately needs to be stimulated to get things going again, so that the person can recover his vitality and achieve an acceptable quality of life; so long as he continues abusing his system, healing cannot work as well as it might.

Even so, Matt's shoulder made good progress over several more healing sessions; although it was still weak because of inactivity, it was now free from arthritis and functioning normally. Mentally, however, he was very confused and unfocused, since he was relying almost totally on drugs for inspiration and comfort. When I again advised him to give them up, Matt retorted that he couldn't see that a stimulant-free life had much to offer him.

I gave him some advice on vitamin and mineral therapy which would at least counteract some of the damage his habits were causing to his body; this advice he did accept. The effects were dramatic; Matt very soon began feeling a lot better. This made him take more notice of what I was saying; by this time, too, we had become good friends and he was not quite so defensive.

As I was still very concerned about him I decided to get much more direct, and during his fourth and fifth sessions

I told him plainly that he must stop taking drugs. Matt's response, again, was: 'What are the alternatives?'

This time, though, he was readier to learn what the alternatives were, and to put them into practice. I taught him some basic meditation and mind-expansion exercises (some of these are included in the last section of the book). Matt was surprised how effective they were; he found them, 'to say the least, incredible, and at last found peace and inspiration from within'. This is how he describes his progress:

> After practice I felt strong enough to cope on my own without stimulants, e.g. drugs and drink, for about four months. [He had one small lapse, after which he kicked his habits altogether.] Throughout this time I felt the real person within me strengthening. I started to see that there is such a thing as self-healing, particularly in terms of releasing mental tension and in understanding oneself.

During the years since, Matt and I have seen each other often as friends, and from time to time I've given him a lecture if he has seemed in danger of lapsing. 'Sorry about that!' I'd say when I was through, and he'd say: 'Oh, no, I needed it!' He has come through with flying colours. In my opinion he has courage and a remarkable non-materialistic side to his nature. He continued his progress by attending my daughter's yoga lessons and has gone from strength to strength. Janet and he have also become firm friends and she has spent a lot of time with him. He has been worth all the effort.

I am sure that the turn-around in Matt's healing process was largely due to his taking the vitamins and minerals I recommended. If people's energies have become very depleted, for whatever reason, it is difficult for them to feel strong enough to be positive. I recommend supplements to most of my patients, usually after the first two or three healing sessions, and I am convinced of their value.

Having been a vitamin and mineral therapist for thirty-odd years, and once considered a crank, I was interested to read, just as I was writing this part of the book, that medical research now shows that proper nutrition and an adequate supply of vitamins can bring about an increase in children's intelligence and improve delinquent behaviour. Of course this has been known in natural health circles for many years.

All true healing must be a whole healing, and to remain totally happy, healthy and youthful as long as possible you must feed yourself properly. Many people who come to me with physical problems like a sprained ankle will tell me they've smoked and drunk all their lives and feel fine. But no one really gets away with it; when I look at them clairvoyantly, I often find that they have blocked arteries without realizing it.

As a very basic guideline I advise cutting out white flour, white rice and white sugar, and eating as much fresh fruit and raw vegetables as possible. Eat white meat and fish rather than red meat; the hormones and other injections given to cattle nowadays are only too easily absorbed into the body. If it's possible to eat unsprayed, organically grown fruit and vegetables, all the better. I also recommend avoiding coffee, which can have harmful effects, particularly on people suffering from depression.

I don't have the time these days to act as a nutrition counsellor, but there are many good books on the subject; those by Adele Davies are excellent, and I recommend them to anyone who is interested in going more fully into the subject of diet. As far as vitamins and minerals are concerned, I can strongly recommend *Nutritional Medicine* by Dr Stephen Davies and Dr Alan Stewart, whose recommendations are in total accord with what I have always practised.

These days it is all the more important to keep our

bodies fit through proper nutrition because there is so much pollution of the environment. For many years now I have been aware of the harm to humanity caused by diseases from outer space. Since I am not a scientist, I realized that nobody was likely to take my views on this very seriously. However, I found them echoed in *Diseases from Space* by Fred Hoyle, a scientist who has always been thirty years ahead of his time.

Today, scientists are concerned about the hole in the ozone layer above the earth, which is allowing too many ultraviolet rays from the sun to penetrate our atmosphere. This could result in an increase in skin cancer, cataracts and other diseases, and an upset in the delicate balance of the world's climate and life-support systems. The cause is now recognized as chemicals from aerosol sprays and polystyrene fast-food cartons! It is to be hoped that some action will be taken on this before it is too late: already the hole in the ozone layer has increased by 15 per cent in the last year.

We must all take some responsibility for the welfare of the planet, as well as for our own welfare. We can all support the earth's natural ecology, even in comparatively small ways: for example by refusing to use sprays of any kind.

It is rare for me to ask people to stop taking medically prescribed drugs. It's not my aim to work in competition with or opposition to doctors; healing should be complementary to conventional medicine. Medical treatment alone may be best for a patient at certain times. For example, I have found that people with serious mental problems generally do best with medically prescribed anti-depressants; I have also found that they can be reassured by explaining to them that the drugs make them feel a little unreal because of their temporary effects on the energy body.

However, if I see that medical drugs or hormones are actually causing serious problems without benefiting the patient, I suggest that perhaps the tablets could be reduced or given up for the time being, while healing is being given. Jenny is a case in point; she is also an example of how a positive personality can help to complement the healing process.

A lovely great-hearted lady in her thirties with her own printing and design studio in London, Jenny used to suffer badly from frequent migraines, accompanied by bouts of vomiting. The fact that she was very unwell when she first came to see me didn't subdue her personality; she's on the large side, and I remember her taking one look at my rather narrow healing-couch and joking about whether she'd fall off it!

Jenny had woken one Saturday with 'a thundering migraine, as usual', but had to go to her office to finish some work for a film première that evening. Too ill to drive, she ordered a cab; the driver happened to be Leslie. She warned him she would have to stop several times to be sick. He was very concerned about her and couldn't believe that she was actually going in to work; when he delivered her to her office he gave her my business card and said: 'Ring this lady. She will sort you out.'

Even though she was feeling half-dead Jenny got straight on to me; she found that even hearing me on the phone made her feel a little better. In fact as soon as Leslie gave her my name and she started thinking about me her mind energy would have automatically come into contact with the healing energies around me. We made an appointment for the following week; in the mean time, I told her to sit quietly for a little while, and relax and breathe properly. Her migraine didn't go immediately, but she did stop vomiting. She came to see me a week later; I'll let her tell you what happened.

> Betty immediately made me feel at ease. She ushered me into her healing-room and asked me take off my shoes and lie on the couch. She told me to relax and

explained that she would place her hands all over my body – starting from the feet – and try to find the cause of these migraines.

Her hands felt very hot and hovered over my tummy. Betty said, 'What are all these scars?'

I explained that at the age of sixteen, I had a thirteen pound growth removed from my womb and that I had had four further operations since then in the same area. In fact, I had just spent a week in a hospital in Wimbledon as a private patient and had been told that after all these operations my body was not functioning properly. I had endometriosis, and had apparently been suffering from it for a long time. It became worse from time to time and caused a lot of side-effects.

I could see that the lining of the womb was in a mess, and very inflamed. When I gave Jenny my diagnosis, she said: 'Thanks! I've just paid a hospital five hundred pounds for that information! And it took them a week to find it out.' Endometriosis is the development of the womb lining, the endometrium, in other parts of the body; nobody knows what causes it, but it can create a lot of pain and misery, and also infertility. Jenny goes on:

I had been taking hormone tablets for about two years and after this last spell in hospital my dosage had been increased. Betty immediately told me that my tummy problems were the root of all my troubles, especially my migraine. I had to laugh, because I had come about my head and in ten minutes Betty had taken me back twenty years to the root of the problem.

At the time I really couldn't work it out, but I kept thinking how the bloody hell did she know about my scars when I was fully clothed?

Well, Betty told me that she would need six weeks

to treat me and I should see her for one hour each Saturday, but she said that she couldn't help unless I stopped taking the tablets.

I knew without any shadow of doubt that, on top of her other problems, the hormone pills were producing an enormous amount of fluid retention. The superfluous fluid was actually pressing on her brain, causing the migraines, as well as making her feel bloated and tired. I didn't think it would damage her health if she stopped taking the pills for a month while we watched her progress; she could always start them again if the healing were not effective. Jenny agreed straight away to stop, but on her way home she started having doubts.

I had been taking these tablets for over two years now and was being treated by a very well-known gynaecologist I had a hundred per cent faith in. I decided then and there that I would go back the following Saturday to Betty, but would continue with my tablets and not let her know. Best of two worlds I thought!

Next Saturday I saw Betty again. Off with the shoes and on the couch.

'Did you throw the tablets away?' Betty asked.

'Oh yes,' I lied through my teeth.

Betty put her hands on my tummy. 'Sorry, but I know you haven't. Your body is still reacting to the tablets and I can tell you are still taking them.'

I felt such a fool being found out, as well as embarrassed at telling lies. Betty laughed at me as I must have looked so silly.

'OK. I promise to stop from today.'

Betty assured me that she could cure me and that I didn't need the tablets. Even though I believed in her I continued to take them for another week.

I thought, 'she'll never know this time.' I think I was frightened to stop taking them – perhaps I subconsciously thought I would start growing a tail.

The following Saturday I was found out yet again. From that day I decided to stop taking the tablets. I put them down the loo.

Two weeks passed and already a miracle had happened. I hadn't had even one little migraine. That alone was a blessing.

On my third visit Betty knew that I really had stopped this time. She said I was steadily improving and that she could work better now.

I remember that Saturday well. After my hour's healing I felt drained and was so tired. I went home and couldn't stop yawning. I went to bed early that night. I woke next morning fresh as a daisy. I had a nice shower and as I was drying myself – my husband said, 'Christ! Look at that bruise. You look as though you have been kicked by a horse!'

Across my stomach and over my right hip was a huge bruise, as big as a dinner plate. Suddenly I felt a bit scared. I knew that I felt OK, but I phoned Betty and explained what had happened.

As usual Betty laughed and said that the healing was working well. She explained that the bruising was a phenomenon that often appeared. I took this in not really understanding it at all, but knowing that something almost magical had taken place.

Jenny's stomach was apparently all colours of the rainbow! Quite why this bruising occurs I don't know, but it has happened so often that I know that it is always followed by a cure. For Jenny:

That was the turning point. I saw Betty on another three following Saturdays and each week she told me how much better I had become. She didn't need to tell me; I was feeling marvellous. My migraine had vanished and my skin was looking great. I felt so much happier and healthier.

I asked her to come back for a booster every six to eight weeks, to ensure that she stayed well. Soon after this last visit, she had her six-monthly check-up with her gynaecologist. 'I went just for the hell of it,' writes Jenny, 'because I had totally forgotten him. I knew I was well – better than I had been in years.'

I went to his private clinic and he checked me externally and internally. He asked me a lot of questions and told me to get dressed and wait until he called me with the result of the test. In no time I was called in. I could tell by his face that he was pleased. He said, 'Well, I am happy to tell you that you are completely clear. I won't stop the tablets, but I will cut the dosage down and you can see me again in six months.'

I asked him if it was the tablets that had cleared my problem at long last. 'Well, yes – but it is very unusual for this complaint to disappear altogether. You must be a lucky lady.'

I told him that I had taken hardly any tablets since I last came out of hospital. I told him exactly what had happened since I met Betty. I was shocked to learn that this was nothing new to him. He made no real comment except to say that the most important thing was that I was well and that I was clear of the problem which had plagued me for twenty years. He never finished writing the prescription.

Five years have passed now and still no sign of the migraine. I have had no tummy pains and I feel extremely well and happy.

* * *

Jenny was worried about her business when she first came to see me. While I healed her I gave her some clairvoyance about her affairs, which gave her peace of mind. A month later my forecast came true and her business recovered from the doldrums. I also knew that she herself was psychic; it's surprising how many of the people who come to see me do have psychic and healing gifts. They don't always follow up on these, but Jenny did: she is now a medium in her own right.

Soon after Jenny got a clean bill of health, I came home one day to find three packages on my doorstep. Inside was a wonderful present from Jenny. She had taken a batch of my poems away, all typed on odd pieces of paper, and had liked them so much that she had printed them in book form. A beautiful way of saying 'Thank you' and my very first book!

As Jenny's case shows, healing can be very effective with gynaecological problems, which can often be solved without resorting to hormone tablets or other drugs, since the chakra system is very closely related to the endocrine system which controls the glands and the natural hormones. I have found that the stimulating effect of healing can help women who have found it difficult to get pregnant. (I have also accurately predicted both the birth-date and sex of a large number of unborn babies!)

I am sure that one reason why Jenny responded so well to healing is that she is always thinking of other people. She has a genuine desire to help others, and this takes the strain off herself; when a person is outgoing and helpful, the mind energy radiates outwards, taking the pressure off the brain and body.

Jenny's attitude is quite different, incidentally, from that of those people who help others because they feel they ought to, and have a guilt complex if they 'selfishly' think about their own needs. It's a difficult line to draw, as their motivation may be excellent; they may be very religious, or anxious to be perfect wives and mothers. But, at the same time, they can be subconsciously objecting to perpetually giving out, and this, too, will affect the energy system and cause illness. (Maggie, whose story I tell on page 204, was this type of woman.)

By contrast, I have come across more than one person who, unlike Jenny, has simply refused to share his or her natural gifts. I remember one woman a few years ago who had been running from therapist to psychiatrist to healer, looking for someone to cure her of her aches and pains and depression. I could see at once that she had the potential to be a healer. But when I told her that the cause of her problems was a build-up of energy that could be used to help others she insisted that *she* had come for help; she felt quite unable to help anyone else because her married life was so miserable.

After talking to her for twenty minutes I discovered that her problems went back to very early in her life, long before her marriage. She came for healing five or six times, which helped to calm her down, but I had to explain to her that if she didn't want to become a healer the excess energies would always cause her problems unless she used them in some way. She took note: when I last heard of her, she was becoming an expert in table tennis, and her 'nervous problems' were receding!

One addiction I haven't so far mentioned, by the way, is an addiction to healing! Receiving healing is so pleasant that many people want to continue when they no longer need it; some would rather go on receiving help than take responsibility for their own lives. But after a number of sessions they really don't need any more. They have received a vast amount of healing energy; their chakras are functioning beautifully, so that they are now drawing in their own life force, and they can continue to heal themselves. I usually suggest, in the nicest possible way, that they should not become over-energized, as this, too, can create its problems; sometimes they only agree with reluctance, but many of them have rung me months later to say they still feel wonderful!

* * *

Stress has become such a popular subject in the media lately that I hardly need tell you that it is widely understood to be a cause or a triggering factor in a large number of diseases, including cancer. Even so, I will repeat it here, because I have found this to be so myself. While there may be genetic, nutritional and environmental factors contributing to ill health, stress is often the last straw; conversely, people can help themselves enormously by learning to be positive.

Worry and fear cause an increase in the production of the hormone adrenalin which, in turn, leads to congested negative energy in the body and the organs are unable to function as they should. Once I have taught people how to relax and use mental exercises, they can usually keep stress-induced diseases at bay.

Stress produced by shock can also be very damaging to body and mind, and healing can deal with it remarkably effectively. If only people would use it preventatively, and go to a healer when they have an emotional shock – just as you might go to a casualty department for a physical trauma – the mind energy would have a better chance of staying healthy and strong. I have also found that many conditions like allergies, asthma and migraines can actually originate with the shock of a difficult birth. In such cases it can be too pat to say that people must help themselves. What they need is the help of a healer who can understand and remove the effects of the birth-shock on the energy system – something it's not exactly easy to do for oneself, even if aware of the need for it!

Shock can have quite serious effects later on in life, too. One day two years ago Alan and I were giving lunch at home to a young student and her parents. Tracy was suffering from epilepsy which had manifested itself in her late teens. Not only was it inhibiting her life, but also the drugs she had been prescribed were having a disastrous effect on her studies.

Sitting opposite her at the table, I took a look at her

mind energy. I asked her to relax, and then explained to her what I could see. The healthy mind energy includes what looks like a series of separate goldish-yellow links, which are not completely joined up but are attracted to each other, probably electro-magnetically, to form a kind of chain around the head. In migraine-sufferers and epileptics there is always a break in these links, and it seems that when a link is broken it's a bit as if a fuse has been blown. I've sometimes told people that they're obviously shorting! In Tracy's case there were two breaks above her head, as if two links were missing. I told her that if she would sit quietly I would link her up.

I looked at her for nò more than two minutes using my 'laser beam' technique to link up the chain. Then, once I saw that this had been done, I told her that she would suffer no more fits. I think both she and her parents found this very difficult to believe! But since that healing she has taken no further drugs and has had no recurrence of the epilepsy.

Afterwards, Tracy felt the physical effects of the adjustment to the electrical circuit around her, and became momentarily very hot and faint. We helped her to an armchair, and in a few minutes she was herself again. I then told her that I had also been given clairvoyantly the cause of her problem: that it had started about two years before as the result of a shock. I asked her if she could remember what it might have been, but after giving it some thought she couldn't recall anything. Neither could her parents.

Later that afternoon, she and I took my dog for a walk, and she told me that she had never got over the death of her own dog, who had been with her for as long as she could remember.

'How long ago was this?' I asked.

'Two years ago to the month,' she replied.

We both realized at once that this must have been the shock I had seen. In addition, she told me that her parents had refused to have another dog; she could understand their point of view, since they would have to look after it, but none the less she was very upset and, without realizing it, had bottled up a considerable amount of grief. The fact that she was able to talk about this to a willing listener completed her healing.

The ability to listen has almost disappeared from our culture; consequently, most of my healing time is spent just listening. Very often there is nothing I can actually do about the problem I'm told about; people's life situations are often so complex, and it isn't my job to interfere. But just listening can be the greatest healer of all, enabling people to get rid of pent-up emotions and release the negative energies that are clogging their systems.

Negative emotions not only cause depression; unless they are dealt with they can produce some very unpleasant physical symptoms. Sometimes the body takes things very literally: I have seen a number of patients suffering tortures with irritating skin rashes, as a result of living with people who irritate them. Resentment and bitterness can result in skin complaints, too.

During the seminar in Segovia I was approached by a young girl whose friends had brought her by car from Madrid especially to see me. Whilst she was talking to me some of her dead relatives came through giving their names and information about the girl and her family. They told me that she had suffered with her health ever since her husband had left her seven years before, and when I asked her she confirmed that this was so. In case you are wondering, the dead relatives were of course speaking in Spanish, but with mind-to-mind communication like this I am also given a simultaneous translation!

She then unwrapped layers of bandages to show me her legs, which were eaten away with painful ulcers. The medical profession had been unable to help her, and with children to look after she was in a desperate situation. My clairvoyant diagnosis indicated that her complaint was psychosomatic; the bitterness she was still experiencing in response to her husband's desertion had caused a physical eating away of the flesh.

She told me she would have no objections to having hypnotherapy in front of an audience, so the next day we appeared together on the platform, with a Spanish interpreter to be absolutely sure she understood everything I said.

I explained the case to the audience, most of whom were medical people, and invited anyone who wished to examine her legs to do so; several of them did. I deliberately did not give her any healing, as I wanted to demonstrate how the power of suggestion could affect the mind of someone in a relaxed state. Of course, healers give out healing energies all the time, so I spent as little time with her as possible. I explained all this to her before we started, and she understood what I was aiming to do.

Despite being the object of so much attention, she quickly relaxed and entered into a hypnotic state. I told her that bitterness was causing her problem, and suggested that she put all thoughts of bitterness out of her mind and to be peaceful and relaxed.

The next day she came to me in great delight; the ulcers had already started to heal, and she was feeling like a different person. Four days later, at the end of the seminar, the doctors examined her again. They could hardly believe their eyes; the ulcers had almost disappeared. Two months later she wrote to me, enclosing photographs showing that her legs were now completely healed.

Whenever I am worried by problems I try to think of this young girl and the state of her legs, and how the condition of her mind was eating away at her flesh. It just isn't worth it!

Negativity is an easy state to get into if you have no one with whom you can share your problems. A lot of people have come to me over the years suffering from depression, and in the majority of cases, somewhere along the line, the root cause is a lack of love. Very rarely do people get deeply depressed about their careers so long as they have a loving relationship. But for those who have no one close in whom they can confide I have included an exercise ('Write It Down') in the final section of the book; I know it can have remarkable results. Try it!

Sometimes I may see that a bad marriage is affecting someone's health adversely; it isn't necessarily helpful for me to say so outright as they may not be in a physical or financial position to do anything about it – nor, of course, do I want to be visited by an outraged husband or wife! In such cases, I usually say that I can see that they are under stress for reasons they will best know themselves, and suggest that they seek outside interests to help them to take their minds off their unhappiness. The companionship and interest of evening classes, for instance, can make a great deal of difference to a person's morale, and remove the mental pressure for at least some of the time.

Motivating people isn't always easy, unfortunately. I can only give people the key to a positive outlook; I cannot make them use it. I know many healers and good doctors who try to take the whole world on their shoulders; in the end you have to give up, because over-concern about one person prevents you from healing so many others.

Every person has to be looked at individually, and sometimes there are changes relating to emotional problems that not only can but also should be made. Maggie, for instance, was a very nice, rather shy woman who came to me with very severe backache and migraine, which I could see were being caused by her marriage. In her case, there was something she could do, particularly when I pointed out to her what I could see and she could not.

I learned clairvoyantly that her husband was a very ambitious man with an overpowering personality, who was 'always right'; consequently, when anything went wrong, Maggie automatically and incorrectly blamed herself. While healing helped her migraines and backache, I knew that for a complete recovery she must stop suppressing her own personality. I could also see clairvoyantly that she would receive promotion in her job, which at the time she didn't think herself capable of. At first, she didn't believe me. I had to talk to her quite a lot to show her that the pent-up tension that she was accumulating was creating her physical problems, and was due to her suppressing her natural emotions.

Gradually Maggie learned to be a little more assertive and to stand up for herself – though always very mildly because she was a naturally gentle person. But the fact that she no longer blamed herself for every domestic difficulty had an enormous effect on her health and her self-esteem. She also began to see her husband and his behaviour with a much clearer eye. Several years later, when he left her, far from being devastated she was quite glad to be rid of him and is living more happily than ever before!

As any psychotherapist will tell you, the causes of many people's problems, particularly people who suffer from low self-esteem, lie a long way back in their childhood. Children feel rather than think; if they feel unloved or insecure, these feelings later become interpreted as thoughts which colour the way they see the world. Then, as adults, they tend to go through life expecting to fail or to be rejected, and blaming themselves when they are.

I have often been able to help people like this by regressing them back to childhood, when their problems first started. Looking back on often misunderstood events with increased understanding, they find that they no longer need their negative self-image. Some people who have suffered as children spend months or years having psychotherapy, but I find that when understanding is combined with healing these traumas can be got over relatively quickly.

As has been shown by experiments with brainwave patterns, the mind energy of the healer takes over that of the client; if the healer is positive – and there's no sense in going to one who isn't – this additional element makes it easier to discard negativity and to start completely afresh without it. At the end of these sessions, I will say: 'Now is when you start living positively! It really doesn't matter a damn what has happened in the past, because you can start again from *now*: now you can start a new life, and when you go out of the door you will be a different person!'

Negativity must somehow be banished. There are many problems that we cannot immediately solve, but we believe that by constantly turning them over in our mind we will somehow find a solution. I have found that this is not the answer, and it causes the mind energy to funnel in even further. But if you *stop* worrying about a problem an answer will usually be given to you quite easily when you least expect it. The old advice, 'Go to bed and sleep on it', makes very good sense. Ten minutes of worry about anything are quite enough; then refuse to think about it any more. In the final section of the book I suggest some exercises for finding your own peace of mind, but one of the best ways is simply to allow yourself to day-dream about something pleasant.

Even watching television can be remarkably relaxing; I have watched people looking at television and seen their mind energies float outwards. Watching the box should never, of course, be a substitute for living; it's much healthier and more positive to go out and do something for yourself. But, if you want to take your mind off things, television can actually be much more relaxing than some formal kinds of meditation, into which some people put so much effort that it doesn't relax them at all!

Best of all, try to cultivate the gift of humour. I believe that those who are born with a genuine sense of humour maintain their own health as well as helping others. Laughter always accelerates healing, releasing negative mind energy; it also helps you to breathe more deeply, enabling oxygen to be carried to all parts of the body. If you can clear your mind of negativity and worries, you will find that gradually your health will improve, your problems will diminish, you will be better able to cope with them and will stand a much better chance of finding your own solutions.

SEVEN

Young Minds

✤

I have worked with a large number of young people, from tiny babies to teenagers, and I have a very high success rate with them. Children's bodies are extremely receptive to healing, and are rapidly stimulated and vibrated back to health. My singer friend Veronica remembers coming away from visiting me and 'seeing a little boy of four being carried in by his father, so thin and frail he couldn't walk by himself, or even lift his head up. Next week I had my visit with Betty and as I left, the same little boy came running in with a basket of flowers and a great big smile. I just stood and stared in amazement. What a miracle – what a gift!'

I love healing children. One of the joys of working with them is that I can introduce them to ideas of positive thinking and self-healing at an early age. This kind of education can set them up for life, and not only in relation to their health. Children are born intuitive; if they are encouraged to stimulate this faculty by using their imagination, they will never lose it. And encouraging a positive self-image from an early age can make all the difference to your child's later health and happiness. It would be wonderful if parents could help their children to use their imagination positively before any kind of ill health sets in, and before their minds are polluted by negative ideas.

Parents are often nervous when they first bring their children for healing. Happily, this doesn't extend to the children, for whom it is a new, enjoyable experience which they accept without question as the most natural thing in the world. They enjoy the sensations it produces, delighting in the feeling of lightness and describing the transference of energy as 'like fizzy lemonade' running up and down their legs! Above all, a healing session with a child is a happy time for both of us, and probably the most rewarding aspect of my job. Children's acceptance and trust are reminders of how things should and could be all the time.

They are particularly intrigued when I tell them about themselves, how they're feeling and their abilities and hopes, and are fascinated that I can tell them how they're getting on at school, and describe their friends and interests. Their eyes light up as they interrogate me as to how I 'do it'. I explain to them in a simplified way how mind energy works, and how the light around their heads grows stronger and stronger the more they learn, until they begin to 'know' about things, about nature, how their parents feel, or if their animals are ill or unhappy – in fact about the growth of their intuition.

Of course, it isn't, strictly speaking, accurate to talk about 'young minds', since mind energy is carried on from one life to another. However, when a mind arrives in a new body it has been, so to speak, 'cleaned up'. In the early years, a child's mind energy expands further outwards and glows more brightly than that of most adults; it doesn't contain the greys and the dark patches caused by accumulated worries. Even in a seriously ill child, the mind energy can glow very brightly. A child's mind is clear, open and receptive. That means that we should be very careful about what is put into it!

Children's minds are extremely suggestible. If a child is constantly criticized or given negative judgements about himself, those suggestions are implanted and may be retained for life, unless the child meets someone who has the power to remove them. That someone doesn't have to be a healer; it may be a caring teacher who will give him self-worth or, as happens very often, a grandparent. Many old people are very good at inspiring children with confidence. While parents want their children to achieve, grandparents can be more relaxed, and say things like:

'Don't worry about your exams. I failed mine ten times, and I made it!'

I myself left school at fourteen, and have gone on learning ever since. Of course, having a link with the universal mind and the ability to absorb knowledge from all manner of minds, I have been able to learn a lot the lazy way! But I would love all young people to be given an understanding of mind energy as early as possible, so that they could grow up using the full potential of their minds.

You cannot give healing to a child too early: in fact most newly born babies could benefit from a healer's touch. Any kind of birth is to some extent traumatic for the child who has to enter a new world with its noise and lights and hundreds of new sensations. If you think about it, at birth the noise alone must be tremendous! The mind of the baby is still close to the dimension from which it has come. During my own visits there, what I have noticed above all is the total peace; even communication is telepathic. Loud or harsh noise is one of the most harmful things for babies and most young children – except, of course, for the noise they make themselves! It is only gradually that their nervous systems toughen up as they grow.

I am certain that an enormous number of 'childish' ailments – such as asthma, eczema, migraines, sleeplessness and other nervous symptoms – have their origins in difficult deliveries. The stress of a traumatic birth creates a misalignment of the energy counterpart, which gives rise to problems which can get progressively worse. Giving a baby contact or absent healing immediately after birth could largely eliminate a number of these at source, saving both mother and child a great deal of stress and anxiety. A very simple alternative would be for mothers or nurses gently to stroke newborn babies, starting at the head and going downwards over the whole body, thus smoothing the energy counterpart into position and settling the mind energy.

Even if they are not dealt with at birth, there are a

number of particularly childish ailments which can be alleviated rapidly and easily in a few healing sessions – problems like asthma, bed-wetting (for which I have found hypnosis very effective), allergies and migraines. Marcus's mother was absolutely desperate when she brought him to see me. He was ten years old, and for two years she had nursed him through headache after headache, watching him repeatedly banging his head against a wall or floor in a desperate attempt to relieve his pain. She had seen numerous doctors who had finally diagnosed the problem as migraine. Giving it a label, however, did nothing to ease his pain.

He would spend weeks off school and suffered many sleepless nights filled with pain, frustration and fear. Although his mother didn't believe in giving him drugs, she had 'pumped him full of Paracetamol' – in her desperation she would have done anything to ease his anguish. She felt the problem must be far more serious than migraine, and she had just decided to see a neurologist privately when a friend told her about me.

When I met Marcus he turned out to be a very lively little boy, although obviously in distress; he was screwing up his eyes and holding his head. I could see that the mind energy had funnelled in to such an extent that it had almost disappeared. No wonder his head hurt! I asked him to lie down and placed my hands on his head: instantaneously, he fell asleep. After some twenty minutes, I began to draw out the mind energy, lifting the pressure from his brain.

Three-quarters of an hour later Marcus opened his eyes, which were now sparkling. His pain had completely gone, he told me, and he exclaimed happily: 'I feel lighter!'

While I was healing him I had picked up the information that he was worried about his maths, so I asked him whether this was so. He told me it was, and that the subject was made the more difficult for him because he hated his maths master. 'I think I can help with that, too,' I told him.

I asked him to lie down again, and this time gave him some hypnotherapy. I told him he should not worry about his master or his maths, that eventually he would actually come to like maths. He enjoyed this session thoroughly; like other young children, it made him feel as though he were flying, and he was able to see lots of beautiful colours.

Marcus only needed two sessions with me; in fact he suffered no further migraines after the first visit. Some six weeks later, I learned that the hypnotherapy had taken effect. Marcus had begun to like not only maths but also the fearsome teacher! I gave healing to his mother, too; she had been very anxious about him, and was at last able to relax. I gave her my booklet on positive thinking, and she has never looked back!

Few people are aware that love and compassion can enable anyone to transfer excess energy to others, particularly those they care about. In the case of mothers this often happens automatically. Unfortunately, the reverse is also true: since babies, children and adolescents pick up vibrations very easily, aggressive parents frequently produce aggressive children. If you are able to put aside your own problems for the love of your baby or your child, you should do so. It is up to parents to give children a peaceful home. Dis-ease within the environment will later become disease within the physical body.

Sad to say, some of the children who come to me are suffering from stress-triggered ailments. From birth, the majority of babies nowadays 'live in the fast lane' with their parents. It is essential that at some time each day babies and small children should be allowed to enjoy a peaceful environment, when everything slows down for a while. This would also, of course, be good for the parents! Television, incidentally, should be kept to a minimum, and should never be used to keep children quiet. I know the temptations, having been through it all myself! However, it does affect their eyes, and the effects of radiation from the set itself, however minute, may build up to produce harmful effects. A much better way to keep a child happy is to give him or her a few more hugs and cuddles – and, above all, have fun together!

I often get calls from parents with children in the throes of acute asthmatic attacks. In practically every case absent healing can arrest these attacks. Asthma is generally regarded as stress-induced, which is not necessarily the fault of the parents; it is very often related to the environment in which they live. This can be an accumulation of things like air and food pollution and bad housing conditions; in addition, if the parents are unhappy about their environment, their children pick up the stress from their mind energy and auras. Despite all these influences, I'm glad to say that I have helped bring about some sixty permanent cures from asthma.

Hyperactivity, which is also related to stress and the environment, I have found rather more difficult to deal with. Food and chemical allergies are often held to blame for this distressing condition, but the causes can be very complex, and may well include genetic factors. I believe that very often one of the parents of a hyperactive child has been hyperactive, or had hyperactive tendencies, so it may well be that a chemical imbalance is being genetically reproduced.

I am afraid there is no single blanket solution to hyperactivity. Working to a busy schedule as I do, it isn't easy for me to go into the subject of food in great detail, though I would always recommend following the basic dietary advice given in the last chapter (page 191). However, I don't believe that hyperactivity is simply related to food; it results from a combination of factors including food, genes, emotions and environment. I feel that these children need individual attention, possibly in a special school where each child could be treated as a separate person. Healing might benefit them if they were given it early enough; when they are smaller they are easier to handle!

I have found some of these children easy to heal, and

some very difficult indeed. One little girl, Fay, was brought to me at the age of eight with two major problems. One was hyperactivity; in addition, she had been born with both her feet turned backwards, and despite a number of operations she still could not walk. Every time she came for healing we could hear loud bangs and cracks, and after each explosion her feet straightened out a little – she used to tell her father I was breaking her bones! However, it was a painless experience.

After six sessions Fay was able to walk up and down the stairs in my home, and became progressively more able to walk unaided every time she came. At the end of each session she was always impatient to try the stairs to see how much she had improved.

Sadly, although by the time of her last visit her feet were nearly completely straight, her hyperactivity became worse, possibly because of some emotional stress during this time. She became totally uncontrollable, and consequently impossible to heal; she was incapable of lying or sitting still enough. Her mother, a very nice woman, did her best to control her, but she had her work cut out as she also had a small baby. In the end we were both forced to give up Fay's healing. This was an enormous shame. I continued to send her absent healing, but I heard no more from her family.

I have healed so many children with so many problems that it is difficult to remember them all. There are one or two, however, who will always stand out particularly in my memory. More than once I have sent absent healing to a child in a coma – absent healing can be very effective, even when the child is in a serious condition. One of these children was Adrian.

One day some five years ago I had a frantic call from the father of a thirteen-year-old boy who was in a coma after being hit by a lorry outside his home. The medical team caring for him had told the father that they didn't think his son would survive – and that if he did it would only be as a cabbage. Unwilling to accept this, he had got in touch with Michael Bentine, who gave him my number.

I immediately made contact with Adrian through absent healing, and received the information clairvoyantly that he would not only recover but would also have all his faculties. I passed this straight on to his father, and also told him that his son had injured his back; I could actually 'see' the injuries and described these to him. At this point the father didn't know what they consisted of, but several days later he was able to see them for himself and confirmed what I'd told him.

I then saw some rapid clairvoyant images which I also relayed over the telephone: one was of the boy with a fishing rod, which was followed by a picture of butterflies. Adrian's father was rather mystified; as far as he knew, his son had never gone fishing or even talked about it, nor did he collect butterflies. In fact he hadn't the faintest idea what I was talking about, and may have wondered how reliable I was! I knew, however, that the source of my information was rarely wrong, so I was certain that these images would somehow turn out to have a connection with Adrian and his family.

As it turned out, on the very day this conversation took place, Adrian's two sisters came home from school, each wearing in her coat a butterfly brooch which their parents had not known they possessed! The father was so astonished that he rang me up straight away to tell me. The meaning of the fishing rod took a little longer to be clarified.

This was by no means an instant healing, and Adrian remained in a coma for some time. About a week after his father first contacted me, his school friends made a tape-recording in the hope that somehow they could get through to him. When the father listened to it at his son's bedside he was shaken to hear them talking about a fishing trip they had planned together.

Playing a tape of familiar voices or favourite music can be very helpful for someone in a coma, and I'm glad to see that it is becoming quite a common form of treatment aid in hospitals. It works, I believe, because sound acts directly on the mind energy. Many people have recovered from comas able to describe what was happening around them while they were unconscious. The mind is obviously all-hearing and all-seeing, even if the brain is not reacting.

My talking about fishing and butterflies might seem totally irrelevant in connection with a desperately ill small boy, but very often evidence like this only seems unimportant until events take place which put it in its true perspective. I knew from experience that these impressions would show that I really was in communication with a source of higher knowledge. Once this was confirmed, it helped give the parents the strength and confidence to carry on throughout their ordeal. In turn, their hopefulness and confidence would have had a positive effect on Adrian's mind.

I continued to give him regular absent healing, and was able to monitor his progress every time I did so; in fact whenever Adrian's father telephoned – which he did daily – I would give him a progress report before he had time to give me one. Adrian's mental recovery was slow at first, but it gathered speed, and after two months he was walking quite well. The last I heard of him, he was going off on a two-week holiday. I lost contact with the family when I moved, but Adrian's father wrote a beautiful letter to Michael Bentine thanking him for the introduction to me, and reporting that with the aid of healing Adrian had made a remarkable recovery.

Of course the medical team were superb throughout, as they always are in these circumstances, but in cases like this other energies are also needed to help bring about a complete recovery. Why not have the best of both worlds?

Another child who stands out in my mind was a little boy of about twelve, on whom my doctor friend Anton worked with me. He had been born with 'trigger' fingers and toes, a condition in which the ligaments shrink and tighten, drawing the fingers and toes inwards. (His mother had a similar condition in her hands, to a lesser degree.) He had had numerous operations since birth and, shortly before coming to see us, pins had been inserted for a time in his fingers and toes in an attempt to straighten them out; none of this surgery did very much for the poor child.

Anton and I gave him healing together every Saturday morning for about eight weeks. During this time, his toes straightened out completely and, as far as we know, they have stayed straight. All his fingers were also perfectly straight except for one that had lesions in it following the operation, which made it very difficult for healing to do anything further; even so, we managed to straighten out the top joint. And there was a bonus: while his mother sat in the healing-room, her own fingers straightened out! We never gave her healing directly; it is simply that healing energy knows no boundaries!

It is possible for healing and surgery to go hand in hand. The story of Nicola is a beautiful example. Nicola Doherty was brought to see me when she was ten years old by her parents: their friend Patrick Moore, the astronomer, came with them. Patrick is also a healer, and very concerned for children.

When she was eight her parents had been told by doctors that Nicola had a progressive heart-muscle disease for which nothing could be done; she could live fifteen years – or just one more. Mr and Mrs Doherty begged for a transplant, but at that time the operation was not suitable for children.

As I gave Nicola healing I was told clairvoyantly that she had always wanted a bird; I asked her if this was so, and she told me it was. I was also able to reassure her parents that she would be fine. After the first healing, Nicola's pale cheeks had acquired some colour, and when she came the second time they were quite rosy! Meanwhile, Patrick Moore bought her a pair of zebra finches, which delighted her.

I gave her four healing sessions in all, after which I continued by sending her absent healing. Healing was not able to bring about a total cure, but combined with hospital care it kept her alive and healthy. Then, when she was twelve, medical technology caught up: a new anti-rejection drug had been developed which revolutionized transplant surgery, so that it could now be carried out on children.

In 1986 the staff at Harefield Hospital told her parents that they wanted to give her a transplant at a time when she was going through one of her better periods. In fact she was so well at the time that Mr and Mrs Doherty had forgotten how desperate they had been for her to have an operation! But of course surgery of this kind is best done when the child is as well as possible, in order to avoid the danger of kidney or lung failure.

The operation was carried out, and was a complete success: Nicola's father now realizes that her good health beforehand was of major importance. Today Nicola is very well – 'absolutely superb', according to her father – and, although she is permanently on anti-rejection drugs, she is living a normal life for a girl of her age. A year after the transplant she had climbed a 2,000-foot hill in the Peak District; twelve months beforehand she couldn't even climb the stairs!

Nicola's one regret is that after the operation the surgeon said she mustn't have birds in the house. Her zebra finches have gone to live with one of her school-friends, so she can still see them. I think it was lovely that at least she had the birds she wanted for a short time!

As Nicola's story shows, healing may keep a child alive and well until the final cure is brought about by medical means. If only people would consider healing as an option early on, many tragedies could be avoided. But, as is so often the case with adults, parents tend to seek the help of healers for their children only when all else has failed, and both parents and children are desperate.

I have been asked whether there is a relationship between cancer and stress in children, as there so often is in adults. I don't think that there is, or that parents should blame themselves for their children's illness. I believe that the causes of so many young people falling ill with cancer are chiefly environmental. In the old days, children were much more stressed, particularly the poor, and they used to die in large numbers of diseases like measles and scarlet fever, but childhood cancer was rare. Although some children had to scavenge in the streets for their food, the environment was not polluted as it is today.

Happily, I have been able to help a number of children and teenagers with cancer and leukaemia – probably around forty in all. Healing can not only help the body to fight the disease; it can also counteract the side-effects of chemotherapy and radiation treatment. For children who are unable to visit me personally, absent healing can still be remarkably effective.

If they can come to me, however, this gives me the chance of teaching them to use mind energy and positivity to fight the disease themselves. Many of them have been quite ill for some time when they arrive; some are very tired and have lost their fight. They may have suffered terribly, being put through blood transfusions, bone marrow transplants, chemotherapy and radiation therapy – but they are extremely courageous and, given the slightest encouragment, they still pop up laughing!

The approach I take is first of all to give them healing to boost their energy; it is difficult to use the mind when one's physical energy is depleted. Then I stimulate their mind energy with games and all sorts of positive thought. Once they begin to laugh, I can really start to help them. When I am teaching them self-healing techniques, I never make it a 'lesson'; I keep it all playful. I pull their legs a lot, and when they come back after a few times they start pulling mine! So we get a lovely rapport.

The actual techniques vary according to the children's age and intellectual capacity but, broadly speaking, I show them how to use their imagination through mental games. They take to these very easily. Unlike adults they don't have to relax deeply first; they can be sitting or lying down, but they don't necessarily have to close their eyes. I will ask them, for example, to imagine a balloon and tell them they can jump into it and float off, feeling themselves getting lighter and lighter. Then I tell them that as they come down they are getting heavier; they actually feel this heaviness. I get them to fly up again, and ask them to lift their legs up to help them to feel lighter. They really feel as if they are getting lighter and heavier, and this helps them to understand the power the mind has over the body.

Then I might ask them to visualize one of a number of scenes, according to their age, illness and character. I might ask a child with a tumour to imagine the animal he or she regards as the most aggressive, and see it attacking their tumour so that it becomes smaller every day. To combat leukaemia I often get children to visualize the cancer cells in the bloodstream being sucked up by a miniature vacuum cleaner. A number of exercises are described in the final section of the book which can be used by both adults and children; children particularly enjoy the one called 'Journey to the Centre of the Universe'. They return with vivid descriptions of people they've passed on the way, obviously inspired by films like *Star Wars*.

Not all children are able to visualize clearly; many of them feel more strongly than they can see. So I ask them, 'Can you see this happening?' and if they can't I will say: 'Well, can you feel it?' So long as they can imagine it, the mind energy will be in action. I also encourage them not to try too hard: the secret of success in psychic exercises is to use as little effort as possible.

When these sick children start practising self-healing techniques they often remark how strong and powerful they are beginning to feel! Imagination, used positively, will do more to strengthen the mind than anything else; once anyone starts visualizing I can always see the mind energy growing in power and strength. I usually see these children's minds expanding so much that it is clear that the energy must be connecting up with cosmic energies and so being revitalized. Stimulating the mind through the imagination also opens up the chakras, which are then able to absorb more life force. Simultaneously, on the physical level, the activity of the mind helps the brain to release naturally occurring painkillers and beneficial chemicals into the bloodstream.

Children enter the world of the imagination so easily that it is rarely necessary for me to hypnotize them; suggestion is usually enough. Occasionally, though, I have used hypnosis with teenagers, some of whom feel it is grown-up to be sceptical. I can overcome that scepticism by giving them the hypnotic suggestion that they won't be able to move one of their arms. When they find their arm won't budge, it makes a great impact!

'That', I tell them, 'shows you the power of the mind! And just as that hypnotic suggestion affected your mind energy, preventing you from moving your arm, you can use mind energy to control what's going on in your body. Every single cancer cell has a mind of its own, and you can control your cells.' They get the message straight away, and we then discuss how to ensure that their cancer cells will do as they are directed, using images that relate to their personal life experience.

With any terminal illness, it would be misleading for a healer to claim that every case could be cured. Sadly, this is not so, and I never raise people's expectations beyond what is reasonable. In fact, parents have often brought along a terminally ill child, telling me: 'We're not expecting a miracle but we feel that we'd like to help him a little.' I myself don't ask for clairvoyant information about the child's future – in fact I block it off, because if I felt there was no hope it would obviously influence my approach. So I always work with the inner assumption that he will recover.

Not all of them do, and it can be heart-wrenching when a child leaves this dimension for the next. Although I know that the mind lives on and the personality of the child cannot be destroyed, I become very close to these children. When one of them dies, I feel I have lost a personal friend.

Children's attitudes to dying are often very different from those of adults: they are more accepting as well as very brave. And their last months or weeks can be greatly eased by healing which, where it cannot bring about a cure, provides other gifts such as peace of mind. In addition, I can use my mediumistic abilities to reassure the older ones. Many of them ask me about life after death and, with their parents' permission, I tell them about the so-called 'dead' people who speak to me, and describe their surroundings, which they find very reassuring. Often 'dead' relatives speak to them through me, and they are delighted when they are reminded of things they used to say or do when those people were alive.

I have had a number of letters from the parents of children who have 'died' telling me how, even when the child has been in a coma, his or her face has suddenly lit up as though he or she has recognized someone. They have been heard to greet by name the person they have seen – a grandmother, perhaps – and have held intelligible conversations with them.

All the children who have 'died' after working with me have come through to me afterwards. They are always happy, and send happy loving messages to their parents. It's lovely to know that, although they are in a different dimension, they still want to make contact with me and through me.

I'm always delighted to work with children in other ways as well as healing. As a medium, I have had the opportunity to guide a number of children towards their natural path in life. Parents, albeit with the best motives, often suffer from a kind of tunnel vision as regards their children's abilities and future career. Unless a child has an obvious natural talent at an early age, like swimming, athletics or music, some parents tend to impose their own ideas whether they really suit the child or not. I don't say this to blame parents: sometimes the child's natural bent is far from obvious. This is where clairvoyant gifts can be a great boon.

Talents are often passed down genetically, but sometimes a gift such as painting may come as a surprise to parents because it is a throwback to a forgotten ancestor several generations earlier, and the genetic strain may come out very strongly in one child. Perhaps a child from a medical family is expected to become a doctor, whereas he or she has inherited from a great-grandfather a talent for acting. That's where, again, I can help by explaining the child's situation to the parents. No child should be forced into a career that does not appeal to him. It is very important to enjoy one's work, and to go on enjoying it throughout life.

In my early days in Sutton I began to acquire quite a reputation for advising mothers who came to me for healing about their children's natural gifts, and a number of them brought their children along for 'vocational guidance'. I remember one ten-year-old boy in particular, because his future path was so clear to me, although it was not at all what an average parent might think of. This little boy was worried about his school work, and his mother wanted to know in what direction she should be guiding him.

I saw David on his own; the poor child was very embarrassed. He didn't really know what he had been brought along for, so I explained: 'Well, what I am going to do is first of all try to find out for you what you are best at doing for a career. And I'm told you're a bit worried about your school work, so I'm going to try to help you with that, too.'

As I was chatting with him I happened to look up, and I 'saw' on the ceiling a full astrological chart, complete with all the stars! I said: 'Isn't it strange? I can see this great big chart on the ceiling. Do you know anything about astrology?'

He didn't, so I gave him a basic explanation and said I

would tell his mother more about it later. I went on to talk to him about his schooling and his future and explained how he had certain abilities inherited from grandparents which he could cultivate. He became very interested and forgot his shyness; he started asking all manner of questions about how I knew what I knew.

As I always do with children, I started by saying, 'I am told,' and went on to explain about mind energy, and how when it is really powerful I link up to another energy from which I absorb knowledge. 'That's how I know,' I said. Children always accept this explanation totally; it makes sense to them.

Then I asked David whether he liked mathematics. 'No,' he said, 'I hate it!'

I said: 'You really must work at your maths because I feel you're going to need it in future.' He just smiled at me; I don't think he really had any conception of what I was talking about, and I didn't say any more to him because he was only very young. But to his mother I said in private: 'David's going to be an astrologer. Do get him on to maths. Don't tell him what I've told you, but get him on to maths because he's going to need it.'

Luckily she took my advice seriously and encouraged him to work at his maths. She must have done it in the right way, because she told me that he became very interested in the subject. The last time I heard from him he was studying astrology.

I have even been able to give careers advice at one or two schools – not on a formal basis, but during the talks I've been invited to give to sixth-formers. I have been asked many times to visit schools to lecture on healing and mind energy, and these visits have been great fun for us all, including the staff! I have thoroughly enjoyed several visits to the boys' public school I mentioned earlier, where I have given demonstrations of clairvoyant diagnosis and healing to the boys and masters. At the end of my talks the young people interrogate me for hours, and sometimes our sessions are hilarious.

I love lecturing to teenagers: their minds are bright and active; they are not afraid to ask questions – nor are they slow to criticize! Through explanation and demonstration I am able to prove to them that there is such a thing as intuition, and that how well it functions depends on the power of their mind energy, and on their ability to relax and allow the mind to expand and travel. Afterwards they always comment: 'Why aren't we taught about mind expansion right from the beginning?' Perhaps the day will come when it will be taught in schools!

I explain that mind energy is strengthened first of all by knowledge. (Of course, positivity is also a prerequisite, but children are *naturally* positive, unless they have been badly treated. It's worth noting that everyone is *born* positive; negativity is something we actually learn!) So I tell them that no matter how they seek knowledge – at school, at home or by reading – their mind energy will strengthen and expand and link up with past masters of the subject they are studying, and plug in, as it were, to their particular cloud of energy.

It takes time, I tell them; there are no short cuts. Whatever the subject at any time, the studying has to be done effectively so that the energy builds up layer by layer. In this way the knowledge they are acquiring will stay there for ever, and won't be forgotten in a year's time. Then, when they have thoroughly learned it, they can afford to relax and allow their minds to wander; when they do this they will also experience the intuitive feeling that they have been given additional information which will manifest itself later, in one way or another – probably the next time they start thinking about that subject. It is the young of today who will have to cope with the world's tomorrows. With developed intuition, it's possible that they will deal with our problems a damn sight better than we have done!

To be intuitive, one has to have a completely open mind and a familiarity with a broad spectrum of subjects. Above all, one needs time to ponder and day-dream, which releases the mind energy so that it doesn't become a captive of the physical. 'Listening to the audible silence' is how I describe this kind of day-dreaming exercise.

One way in which I demonstrate my own clairvoyance is to describe to each one his natural talent. If young people are helped to recognize their talents early in life, they can at least have a go at nurturing them. Sometimes, of course, a child's gift may not be one from which he or she can make much money. Healing is a good example! In that case I would encourage them to cultivate their interest as a hobby which they can continue to enjoy through life.

My friend Louise is a particularly open-minded head teacher, and it has now become a regular event for me to talk with her sixth-form girls. At this age they are not going to be taken in by anybody; they can be extremely challenging, and we have some lively discussions! At the end of the talk I go round the thirty or forty girls and tell each one about her personality, her potential and her natural talent. Nearly all of them, interestingly, have already chosen a career which is in line with what I tell them. And their classmates find the descriptions of their personalities very accurate.

Louise has commented that my readings of the girls' characters are always couched in very helpful language, so that although I may be saying quite personal things in front of the others they don't cause embarrassment; I am always careful to make factual comments, but not to criticize. She says that the staff find this session helpful, because although they know the girls well 'the encounter somehow draws out a very clear and fuller picture of each girl, sometimes showing sides of them or even secret hopes of theirs that they didn't know about; so they learn more about the girls.' It is possible that we shall start doing this with younger classes so that the staff can get to know the girls in depth at an earlier stage.

Louise also comments: 'I think some of the other more

general things Betty says are very helpful, for example about the Law of the Universe – that what you give out you get back – and how you affect other people. That all makes a lot of sense to the girls.' I, too, have noticed how this message seems to strike home particularly to the young.

Although I'm happy to guide young people in this way, I do discourage them from seeking clairvoyant sittings, which can be negative and lead to non-action. I much prefer to teach them to be self-reliant, to make up their minds what they want to do, and go for it!

Teenagers can be rather sceptical, and like to test you. One young woman of seventeen or eighteen asked me what she should do in life. I knew that she already knew perfectly well, so I simply said: 'Well, what do you want to do?'

She laughed, and said: 'I want to be a theatre director.'

I said: 'But you have a natural genetic propensity towards that, haven't you?' She looked rather taken aback by that. Afterwards, Louise told me that the girl came from a theatre-owning family!

These girls are privileged, and I am aware that many children face prospects of unemployment when they leave school. This is where positivity is terribly important: no young life needs to be wasted. It is hard for unemployed teenagers to feel they can't get jobs, but they do have that very precious commodity, lots of spare time, which they wouldn't have if they were working. That time can be used to teach themselves subjects that could eventually lead to a much better career, and will certainly make life more interesting. Learning, studying, acquiring any kind of knowledge will strengthen their personality, expand their mind and their intuition, and make them more desirable candidates for jobs. If only they knew it, older people are quite envious of all that spare time, and wish they had the time to learn a language or study.

Some people suggest that the young unemployed should do voluntary work to help others, but I feel that is only appropriate if they are naturally compassionate – and compassion is rare among the young; you have to have a lot of spots knocked off you before you develop it! Youth is the time for learning.

In my exchanges with young people I have come across many potential healers, but healing is not a career I would recommend to the young, who need – as well as learning – to enjoy themselves and acquire experience of living. But it can be developed to use in their spare time, and there are some suggestions as to how to pursue this interest in the final section of the book.

I am also aware that a large number of psychic children are being born today. This is particularly the case in Britain, where we have been going through a transformation scene of late which is currently gathering speed and power. In the past, children like myself who saw and heard things that other children didn't were accused of making things up, lying, or worse. Today, it's reassuring that some mothers are accepting that their child may indeed be telling the truth. For about a century now people have been practising and teaching mediumship and healing, and other people have listened and absorbed their teachings, even if they don't always agree with them. This has opened up the way genetically: everything that goes through the mind affects the body, including the genes, of the next generation.

Very often psychic abilities are passed down from grandmother to granddaughter, as they seem to have been in my own case. But I think my present family must be very unusual, if not unique, in having psychics in three generations at once! Not only is Janet very psychic, but so is her daughter Raina, who is seven years old at the time of writing.

Some nine years ago Janet was going through a divorce and was very depressed. One day I suddenly had a vision of her walking with a little girl of about three; I instinctively knew this was her child, and I told her she would be having a little girl in two years' time. At the time, there was no other man on the horizon and this was the last thing Janet wanted to hear!

Two years later to the month Janet, now happily remarried, gave birth to a beautiful baby girl. When I visited her and baby for the first time I said: 'My God, Janet, that baby is psychic!' Janet responded rather crossly: 'Oh, Mum! You think everyone's psychic!' Which isn't true!

When Raina was about six months old I was impressed that she would be very artistic and would become an actress. When I told Janet, she said that Raina's father had very positive ideas about her future, and wanted her to be a doctor. I laughed and said: 'She won't heal anyone.'

Janet and her husband were rather annoyed, as they had made up their minds. However, at the age of eighteen months Raina was singing, and when she was two she announced: 'I want a biolin.' No one in the family plays a violin, and she had never seen one played, so we feel that this must be the result of a past-life memory. Raina now plays the violin, sings, dances and acts all the time. She is also very psychic.

When Raina was two she astonished Janet by telling her: 'There's a lady in that chair, smiling at me. Come and see her.' She took her mother by the hand to meet the lady. Janet could see no one – her psychic gifts do not include seeing spirits – but she was aware of a presence, and was positive that it was my mother, who did have a lovely smile. Another time, Raina drew Janet's attention to a 'man' standing by the window; again Janet could see no one but was aware of a presence. Raina stood happily smiling at the man – her visitors always seem to be friendly.

On several occasions Raina has been able to tell us what was in a sealed envelope or parcel. On her fifth birthday, we handed her an envelope and before she opened it she said, 'This is a teddy-bear card,' which it was. Another time, I had bought her some Mickey and Minnie Mouse pyjamas, with a T-shirt style top. Before giving them to her, I asked: 'What do you think I've got for you, Raina?' Promptly, she answered: 'Mickey and Minnie Mouse T-shirt!'

Recently, she told Janet: 'There's a man upstairs; he's smiling at me. He told me his name was Herbert. Come and see him.' Apparently, she had seen him in her bedroom before. Janet, feeling rather guilty, but knowing she wouldn't be able to see the man, told Raina she was too busy. Later Alan told us his father's name was Herbert; neither Janet nor I had known this. Wanting to check it out, I asked Janet to ask Raina what the visitor had looked like, but Janet refused, saying: 'I don't want to make it seem important.'

Janet accepts what Raina has to say without making a big issue of it, and we don't discuss my work or psychic matters in front of her. Raina is fortunate in having her feet planted very firmly on the ground, but if her gift ever became a problem she has a family who could explain things to her, keeping logic firmly in the foreground. She also comes out with some extraordinarily wise and spiritual statements, which simply don't sound like the comments of a seven-year-old; I feel sure she is being taught and guided, just as I was.

I think that Janet's low-key approach is exactly the right way to handle the situation. If your child starts telling you about people who aren't there, he may be using his imagination, or may be genuinely seeing spirit people. In either case, it can only damage the child's natural creativity and intuition to tell him 'not to make up stories'. It is in the psychic child's interests not to be made to feel 'different'; indeed, many of these children lose the gift around the age of seven. The best way to deal with invisible visitors is to say to your child, 'That was interesting, wasn't it,' and then forget it.

Conversely, I think it is a big mistake to *encourage* the psychic gift and treat the child as a prodigy. The psychic world is hard enough for adults to cope with! Allowing children to experiment with things like ouija boards I would absolutely discourage, as they can attract negative energies.

Psychic children should, above all, be treated as *normal* children, and have plenty of fun in their lives. If they have a genuine gift, it should be allowed to develop naturally — which it will anyway — without imposing any preconceived ideas. In my own case, I've always been grateful that I was separated at an early age from my spiritualist grandmother, so that I was not affected or influenced by her. It is so important to be self-reliant and discover the truth for yourself. I really do believe that everything I have been taught, to the point where I was shown the existence of mind energy, has come direct from a higher source. That is how the best education takes place!

EPILOGUE

Expanding Your Mind

✺

Let us endeavour to live so that when we come to die even the undertaker will be sorry.

MARK TWAIN

While this book has been largely about my work, it is my hope that it will make an impact on its readers' minds and lives. Everyone has the potential to expand his mind energy and use it more creatively and positively. This chapter is dedicated to you. It includes mental exercises which you can practise to have fun with, to experiment with, and to expand your mind with. Remember that the mind *is* energy: it should be allowed to flow like the sea, back and forth like the tide.

PRACTISING POSITIVITY

Positivity is the only way to achieve a free mind. When you are being positive, your mind flows easily and automatically. Let me remind you that when you are negative it is drawn inward, causing compression on the brain and body. Both positivity and negativity are self-generating: positivity creates further happiness and optimism; negativity can only lead to unhappiness and pessimism. When you are depressed the negative energy compresses the brain, making it unable to function properly: thinking becomes muddled, and the chemistry of the brain alters.

The easiest way to think positively is *not* to think negatively. If your problems cannot be solved at once then, after peaceful logical consideration, shelve them until a solution can be found. Don't make them worse by churning them over in your mind! Instead, try the exercises in the next few pages.

After all, you are in control of your mind – no one else; the answer lies within *you*. As you cultivate positivity you take greater control over your own destiny. Natural talents that you may have neglected begin to come to the fore. Decisions become easier. Life itself becomes easier. You can control your emotions and nobody, but nobody, can shake your equilibrium.

It is not easy at first to reach a positive peaceful frame of mind all the time, and if you happen to be a natural worrier it can be quite difficult! But I assure you that the direction of your mind *can* be reversed. Always give yourself a long break from thinking about anything negative, until it finally leaves of its own accord. If you fail, don't dwell on your failure: have another go, and another, and another. Keep trying, and eventually positivity will become part and parcel of your whole being. You will in fact become a *whole human being*.

Relationships with others may come and go, but you will still always be yourself – happy and carefree. You don't have to be a saint: there will always be some people who will make you angry, sad, frustrated – momentarily. That's natural. But if you have a negative response don't allow it to continue and spoil your life. Get rid of your pent-up feelings by writing them down (see page 237). And let them go.

Other people will make you happy – that is a bonus. But you will still be a whole person, sharing your joys with others, but not dependent on them for your happiness.

Once you have acquired the art of positive thinking, you will never *want* to go back to negative thinking. The happiness you will have attained will be so beautiful that you will never want it to escape you again.

Never be afraid of anyone or anything. Fear destroys the ability to think for yourself, to act logically and make important decisions. Fear can make you a prisoner of someone else's mind, instead of having the courage to say what you really think. So never hide behind others for fear of the consequences of speaking up. And don't allow anyone else to draw up a blueprint of what you should or should not do or be. Be courageous and make up your own mind about what you want and need from life.

Only you know what you want: it may not be what your partner or friends want but, unless you fight for what you know is right for you, you will not progress. Even if you consider your daily life to be dull, your uniqueness makes it interesting: there will never be another you! So never regard yourself as unimportant. Trying to please others and walk in their footsteps can only lead to unhappiness for both parties. Have the courage to follow the path of your own truth and positivity. Practise every day.

Never be envious of anything or anybody: envy is another totally destructive and negative emotion. You have tremendous potential within you, once you have acquired the habit of positive thought. *You* can attain similar heights and similar achievements in your own individual way. The rewards are there: the brain, released from its prison of compressed energies, can function fully. Your mind, once freed, can go forth and join the universal mind, returning to you with clarity of vision and an intuitive knowing of where you are going and what you are capable of achieving. The rewards for positive thought are immense – an adventure that will last the rest of your life.

The most terrible of all negative emotions is hatred. If someone has hurt you badly, put it down to experience and let it go. If we do not experience all the human emotions, we do not progress: so acknowledge your hatred, and feel it, but don't hang on to it. Dwelling on it will draw the energies inward and down into the subconscious. When you realize the damage this causes to your brain and body, you will want to dismiss the feeling immediately.

Greed is another emotion to avoid. Most people don't need three-quarters of the possessions they work like maniacs to own! Human beings do like to hoard; no harm in that. But, if possessions or success don't come easily to you, go without rather than build up a stressful situation trying to achieve the impossible. When you allow your mind to be free, you will be surprised how very much easier it becomes to attract these things.

. All life is a challenge. Once you acquire a new optimistic outlook, nothing will be able to stop you. The mind, now free, will ebb and flow as it joins the universal mind. Your intuition will be second to none. Intuitively, you will be doing and saying the right things. Everything will flow easily and naturally, ebbing and flowing with nature and the universe, at one with all the dimensions. With expanded awareness you will link up to a cosmic driving force that will be behind your every activity, be it work or play. Follow your intuition, don't argue with it. You'll be surprised how right you can be.

And if you do something wrong, then be *positively* wrong and enjoy it! While I always discourage negative emotions, it's much healthier to acknowledge that they are there: then you can do something about them.

SOME EXERCISES FOR GETTING RID OF NEGATIVITY

Dealing with Depression

A very simple way of dealing with depression is to allow yourself five minutes of negative thought at a time, and then simply switch off! It's difficult at first, but it is possible and becomes easier with practice.

How often have you dwelt on a difficult situation, and found your thoughts snowballing? The longer you allow this to go on, the larger the snowball becomes. Why not melt it down in a surge of energy, by replacing the negative with the positive? Feel yourself becoming lighter as the mind energy is pushed upward and outward and connects with universal energies.

You can do it; you *must* do it. Depression is unhappiness, and you don't need it. There is quite enough misery in the world; you can help by refusing to create any more. However small, your effort is important. It will affect those you live with and work with, making their lives a lot easier and happier. They in turn will pass this on, until everyone is creating vital positive energies around them.

If other people upset you, the same rule applies. Don't dwell on it. Think about it for a maximum of five minutes, then switch off! You may find those five minutes becoming four, and then three, and then two – and finally you'll find that you can recover your equilibrium in one minute!

Write It Down

Another way of getting rid of depression and other negative feelings is to get paper and pen and write everything down. Unhappiness, hatred, envy, despair, jealousy, resentment, vindictiveness – let all the problems that have been building up tumble out of your mind on to the paper!

Don't be afraid to own to these feelings. You are not alone; all these and more are natural feelings that tend to surface during our lives when circumstances trigger them off.

Keep writing your feelings down until you are sick of writing. Whatever you do, *don't* read through what you have written. Let it go. We are rather like computers, and reading the information would store it again. Tear the paper up into small pieces and put them in a container such as a biscuit-tin. Then set light to the paper, preferably in the fireplace or garden (if you haven't either, use the sink where you can turn the tap on if necessary!) Reduce the whole thing to ashes, and start your life afresh.

This is also an excellent way of getting rid of all the things that you'd like to say to other people, but don't dare say or don't want to hurt them with. Say them on paper, and finish with it.

You don't need all that rubbish; allowing it to build up inside you will only lead to illnesses of mind and body. Cleanse yourself of unnecessary burdens. We acquire so many that this clean-out is an absolute must, at least once a month! It will help you to be in control of your life.

Above all, enjoy it. It can be great fun!

Time on Your Hands

So many people are unemployed at the moment, including the young, that I'd like to give them this special message.

Time is something which, when we are busy, we never have enough of. Yet when we do have it, it is so easy to waste! Rather than spending it feeling depressed, people with time to spare could help themselves to a happier future by studying and learning as much as possible. Evening classes are cheap, or if this isn't your style you can borrow language tapes and books from the library – languages always come in useful. You don't have to be good at English; many people who have studied a second language have been able to conquer the grammar better than they did their own!

Using your spare time could, in the long term, enable you to take up a better career when the chance comes along. With more knowledge, you'll have more choices.

Time is precious. Please don't waste it!

EXPANDING YOUR MIND

For our health and happiness, we have to become aware of the energies that surround us. We must learn to acquaint ourselves with knowledge that we have forgotten and yet lies dormant in our souls. Have you ever thought, as many people do, that you would like to strip yourself of material trappings and sit alone on the top of a mountain and just be? These yearnings are common because within ourselves we know that spiritually we are missing out. It is necessary for human beings to feel the wind and rain and touch the earth, communing with the forces of nature, and just as necessary to harness unseen energies for our needs. There is a vast unseen world, like an iceberg whose tip we have only glimpsed.

We are all capable of tapping that vast sea of energy which, I believe, is created by the minds of people in other dimensions. We can do this by expanding and strengthening our own minds with knowledge, and by meditating in our quieter moments.

In this section I am going to teach you some of the exercises which I ask people to do at home. I prefer people not to do formal types of meditation, which can be too focused; if you practise them wrongly or with too much effort, or are fanatical about doing so many minutes at the same time every day, the aura actually closes up instead of expanding!

In my experience the finest form of meditation is day-dreaming. In allowing the mind to wander to places where it wants to go, you are not *trying* to be spiritual or trying to be anything else. You are simply relaxing and enjoying yourself. However ill a person is, they can always day-dream, which projects the mind energy away from the body, and lifts the compression on the brain that causes depression.

Always project thought outwards. As well as using your imagination, take opportunities to walk or sit outdoors, and look at trees and the sky.

All the following exercises are designed to exercise your imagination; imagination stimulates mind energy, which in turn revitalizes the whole body. Remember that the less effort you put into it the further your mind energy will travel.

At the start you may find it helpful to make your own tape from the written description and play it so that you can go through each stage slowly and peacefully. Going through it slowly will ensure that it will be maintained in your subconscious. As you become more adept, you will need less and less time to go through the exercises.

239

Never spend more than ten minutes on any exercise — you can get turned on to turning off!

Preparation for Mental Exercises

Before practising any of these exercises, it is essential to make yourself completely peaceful. If you are indoors, disconnect the telephone and turn off anything else that is likely to ring or jar you in any way. If you have animals, shut them in another room.

Now, sit in a comfortable chair and relax. Breathe deeply and slowly, and allow your mind to wander.

Think yourself, in the most relaxed way, to a place of peace. It could be by the sea, in a sunlit meadow, on top of a mountain, beside a river, or anywhere where you know you would feel happy and peaceful.

Every time you practise, really enjoy the experience and use your imagination to build up this feeling of peace. Feel the waves lapping at your feet, count the species of flower, breathe the mountain air, or watch the sun sparkling on the water. Remember there is no limit to the expansion of the mind.

Feel yourself floating along. Do not put any effort into your imagining; this will only create tension. In fact the less effort you make the more effective it will be.

Journey to the Centre of the Universe

I remember looking up at the stars at an early age as though I depended on them for knowledge. Over the years I have continued to look out into the universe, asking questions to which no one here has been able to provide the answers.

This exercise is designed to encourage your mind to expand and develop your intuition and will also help you to heal yourself. Try to practise it at least once a day.

Start as in the previous exercise by sitting quietly; breathe deeply, and relax.

Now visualize a small spacecraft for one person – it could look like a small racing car – with a transparent cover. Get into the spacecraft and pull the cover over you, sealing yourself inside. It is air-conditioned; as you travel you will be able to feel jet-streams of cool fresh air, which will be with you the whole time. Relax, feel safe and secure.

Now feel yourself being lifted off the ground by a gradual build-up of energy, until you find yourself travelling through the universe. As you go along you will pass galaxies of stars. Stay relaxed, noting with interest everything you see.

In the distance you see a small white light, which becomes larger and larger until it eventually fills your horizon. When you reach this light you can see a tunnel in it. Your spacecraft automatically enters this tunnel.

After a short journey you arrive in a large hall with a domed ceiling. A friend or guide will be there to meet you; trust your imagination to give them the appearance that is right for you. He or she takes off the transparent cover of your craft and helps you out. Relax. Now your guide takes you to a room in which a blue haze is flowing back and forth: this is healing energy.

You then take a seat in the centre of this room, where you will feel yourself absorbing this energy. If you have any particular ailment, feel the affected part of your body absorbing the energy, and the ailment leaving you and disappearing.

After a while your guide takes you to a large room in which a group of wise people are seated in a semicircle. You will sit in the centre opposite them. You will be aware of a feeling of total peace and contentment, and you will know that you are absorbing knowledge telepathically from these spiritually progressed people. Don't expect at this point to know what you are being told; the information will manifest itself when it is needed.

After a while your guide will lead you back to the large domed hall and help you into your spacecraft, fastening the cover securely over you. The craft will be guided through the tunnel and back out into the universe. You will feel the pull of earth's gravity, and you will return safely, landing upon layers of energy to be let down lightly to the place you started out from. Get out of your craft and find somewhere to be quiet and peaceful for ten minutes.

The Balloon

I have taught this exercise to many terminally ill adults and children; it has helped most of them to die peacefully, as it has enabled them to let go of the physical and melt into the universe. If you are fighting fit, you can still use it as a superb exercise for total relaxation.

Sit or lie down, breathe deeply and relax. Now imagine that you are getting into the basket of a hot-air balloon. Children who do this exercise often imagine getting inside the balloon itself, which is fine.

Feel the balloon leaving the ground; feel the sun on your face and the warmth of the atmosphere relaxing the whole of your mind and body. Let go!

As you travel higher and higher, you will find any pain and discomfort becoming less of a burden. Let the balloon travel for about five minutes, taking you wherever it wants to go.

When you want to return simply think yourself down, and you will feel yourself gradually sinking lower and lower until you touch the ground.

The Auric Egg

There are times when we can't avoid living or working with people who are antagonistic towards us, or whom we find difficult to get on with. This exercise is a safe method of protecting yourself from unwanted outside influences. It closes the aura, and prevents it from absorbing influences from other auras.

242

First of all, imagine a large egg – large enough for you to walk into. There is a door in it: go through the door and, once inside, fill the oval floor with cushions, so that you have a level surface. Sit or lie down, close your eyes, and relax.

Now, visualize the outside of the egg, the shell, growing harder, including the door. Be sure not to put any effort into this; just *know* that, as you think it, it is happening. Watch the shell becoming impenetrable, and when you are satisfied that nothing can get through, stop visualizing and relax for about five minutes. Then you can get up and carry on with whatever you have to do without any worry. This is a good exercise to do if you have to travel on crowded tube trains, too.

Smoothing Your Aura

Ever since I saw my own lopsided mind energy in the mirror, I have regularly treated myself by smoothing out my aura. Anybody can do it. Using both hands, simply stroke downwards over your head and the area around it, and then stroke down over your shoulders. You can use a soft scarf held in both hands to do your back. Then use your hands to smooth down each arm in turn, going right over the ends of your fingers, and then stroke down your body, legs and feet. This also removes toxins lying just under the surface of the skin.

Mind Medicine

This is a positive way of controlling anxiety in times of illness or stress. It can be used to complement ordinary medicine or, in the case of minor ailments, enable you to do without it altogether.

First step: Carry out the first-step relaxation exercise.

Second step: Imagine a corridor, not too long; at the end of it you will see a door, which can be any colour you choose. On this door you will see your name printed, and underneath it the words 'MIND MEDICINE ROOM'. Only you possess the key to this door. Insert the key in the lock and go in, locking the door behind you.

On entering, you will see the room of your choice, not too big and quite cosy. All along the walls are shelves and drawers, and tables with cupboards beneath them. There is also a big comfortable armchair, and an incinerator for rubbish. This room is entirely your creation: if you see anything in it that you don't like, alter it to suit your particular needs.

Third step: On the shelves and inside the cupboards and drawers you will find a huge selection of bottles, phials, pots and other containers for potions, lotions, creams, tablets, a container full of cotton-wool balls, and anything else you may need for treating yourself. You can choose the colours and shapes of these receptacles.

Remember that if you are under par you are not as clear-seeing as when you are well. So it would be advisable over the next few months whenever you enter this room mentally to make out your own labels for the receptacles. Write clearly so that you can 'see' exactly what the contents are. For example, you could include a box of 'Headache Tablets', a jar of 'Antiseptic Cream', a tube of non-harmful 'Pep-Up Pills' for when you need extra energy, some non-addictive 'Tranquillizers' (maybe herbal ones) for when you want to be calm, and 'Sinus Fluid' in a wide-topped jar that you can inhale from. Whatever your label indicates will automatically be inside the container. Whenever you need something you haven't already got, you can add it immediately. Create your medicines according to your own needs: diabetics doing this exercise have made their own supply of insulin. Make these medicines as real as you can; feel them and sniff them – you may find you can actually smell them.

Then you can use the contents in the following way.

Fourth step: Let us imagine that you have injured your knee and the inflammation around the injury is very painful. Go to the jar which you have already labelled

'Antiseptic Cream' (or label a jar if there isn't one there already). Unscrew the top and put some of the cream on your knee. Watch it as it turns red, absorbing the inflammation; then wipe it off with cotton-wool, and burn this in the incinerator.

Keep repeating this action – putting on the cream, watching it absorb the inflammation, and throwing the cotton-wool into the incinerator – until the cream no longer turns red. Then leave the remaining cream on your knee.

Put the top back on the pot, the lid back on the cotton-wool jar, make sure everything is spotlessly clean, and then sit down in the armchair. You now know in your *mind* that you have started the process of self-healing. You have released into your body the chemicals necessary to ensure that the process works.

When you feel you have rested enough, go back to your real-life room and carry on with whatever you need to do next. If you are doing this exercise in bed, you can now go straight off to sleep.

Do not wait until you are ill or injured before training yourself in this exercise. If you become adept at it while you are well, when you are really in need your recovery will be automatic and speedy. Practise it every day; it works! You will find you need fewer and fewer visits to the surgery; and even when you do have to see a doctor you will still find this method supportive.

You can use this to control panic situations such as heart palpitations or an asthma attack, by giving yourself immediate first aid from your supplies of medicines.

This exercise works by encouraging the body to manufacture the chemicals it needs for self-healing. It really works – some diabetics have become so good at this that they have been able to reduce their medical insulin intake by encouraging the pancreas to produce its own.

Try it for yourself, and teach your children how to treat themselves for minor injuries. They will grow up to be healthier and more self-reliant. Above all, enjoy it! It could change your life.

Healing Yourself through Colour

Colour is a powerful aid to healing and self-healing. You may naturally find colours coming in when you are doing any of these exercises, or you can deliberately imagine beams of coloured light playing on you while you are relaxing or going off to sleep. In imagining these colours you can actually bring cosmic colours in to help and heal you.

Particular colours benefit particular conditions. Green is calming and relaxing, very good for nervous tension; red will energize you and strengthen you; it is also good for removing the pain of arthritic complaints – but don't use it if you suffer from overactive adrenalin glands and excessive acidity. Yellow is good for alkalizing acid conditions. Blue is the perfect healing colour for almost every condition; it produces a very peaceful and fluid feeling, as if a wave of water were flowing gently over you.

Purple is a very special colour, which seems to come in naturally when people are very spiritually progressed; it has very powerful healing energies, especially in cases of excess adrenalin. White is also very powerful for healing, since it contains the full spectrum of colour; I find that it is brought in when I have patients with serious conditions like multiple sclerosis and cancer.

Don't worry too much about getting the 'right' colour; the colour itself is less important than what you believe it means. There is no doubt that we attract what we need; when I have asked people to think of a colour they have sometimes told me that, for example, they wanted to visualize green but kept getting blue. This shows that as soon as your imagination starts to expand your mind energy you are able to link up with other dimensions and are given the colour that you need. The more you trust your intuition, the more reliable it will become!

If you want to experiment with colour healing, even with no healing ability, you can learn a lot from an excellent book by S. G. J. Ouseley, *The Power of the Rays: The Science of Colour Healing*. It is a mine of information about both colour and the chakras.

Healing

It is often said that everybody is psychic, and that everybody can heal. This is probably true, but becoming a full-time psychic or healer is another question. I know that there is an increasing number of development circles and training courses available today, but my personal belief is that if you are destined to be a healer you will not need to chase after the gift – it is much more likely to chase after you!

Professional full-time healers need to have a great deal of healing power, or they will find themselves unable to help the more seriously ill. If anyone intends taking up healing as a career, they should first of all ask themselves if they want any other kind of life, because healing does require total commitment. I don't think that young people should consider it, as it is important for them to live their own lives. Very often, the necessary compassion is developed only after living through a great deal of personal grief and many problems. (I also believe that this stress enables the healer's chakras to be abnormally wide open, so that they are drawing in and giving out life force all the time.)

There is nothing, however, to stop anyone giving healing to their friends and family. Think about it: when a child or family member is ill, it isn't only drugs and medicine that makes them well, it's the care and attention and love that their friends and relations give them. Love and compassion open up your chakras, allowing extra life force to come in, for you to give away to those you care for.

What I would like to get over to you is the simplicity of it. You can read books and do exercises to open and close the chakras: in my view, there's only one thing that will open the chakras and that is compassionate love. When you stop thinking about yourself, and start wanting to help another person, your mind expands, your chakras open, and very often you can feel the extra life force coming in. If you use your hands, allow them to be guided intuitively; but whether you lay your hands on the person, or simply *think* healing in their direction, you will be healing them.

Anyone can send absent healing to those they care about. The best way is to say simply, 'Please help', and then *know* that help is being given. At the same time imagine that you are telling your friend telepathically: 'I have asked for help and you are receiving help.' That's all you need to do; *that thought is the deed!*

It's very important to realize that putting any effort or force behind it closes up your mind energy so that it can't travel to its destination. When I have been teaching groups how to do this, my chief difficulty has been getting over to them how not to put any effort behind it.

The first time we try it, I often see their mind energy go out only so far, and then stop. I smile and say: 'You're really trying hard, aren't you! Well, *don't!*'

They look at me, somewhat shocked, and I have to explain that I appreciate how difficult it is to control their enthusiasm, but that it's actually blocking the energy. Then, as soon as they stop trying, I can see their mind energy shooting outwards. Remember, the less impetus you put behind the thought, the faster it travels.

Some people also teach quite complicated exercises for closing down the chakras after healing. It is certainly important to be very well earthed if one is going to use healing or psychic gifts, but there are some very simple ways to bring this about. Any normal, natural and down-to-earth activity will automatically close down the chakras, like making a cup of tea, or doing the washing-up. Gardening and writing are also excellent; so is a thought like 'I must pay my electricity bill!' which can bring you to earth more quickly than anything!

These earthing activities are particularly important, of course, if you do have an excess of life force and *don't* want to use it in healing. (Some of the signs of this are feeling very hot, faintness and wobbly legs, and tingling sensations in your hands.) Here are some further ways you can use excess energy, or test and develop your powers.

ENERGY GAMES

I have done a lot of experiments with psychic energies, some purely for fun. I think the following energy games will amuse you and perhaps, most of all, encourage those of you who believe you have the gift to try some experiments for yourselves. They may not come out the way you expect!

Although I have given up these experiments, preferring to devote all my energies to healing, they were a useful training and they proved to my satisfaction that there are many elements in energy that we know nothing about.

Water into Wine

I tried this at a time when I had been working very long hours and decided to have a complete day's rest. As my mind is very rarely inactive, I thought I would encourage it to enter a meditative state by focusing it on something novel. After much thought, I decided to devote the whole day to seeing whether I could turn water into wine!

Making sure I would not be disturbed, I sat the entire day at the kitchen table with a wine-glass full of water. I put my hands around the glass, and wafted off into dream-world – which wasn't difficult, as I was so tired. At the same time, I kept in my mind the image of the glass filled with red wine.

Two hours after beginning, the water had become quite warm under my hands but, to my disappointment, was still water. I made myself a cup of tea, then sat down again, putting my hands back around the glass, and drifted off again, still keeping the visualization going.

Another two hours, water still water, but very hot indeed. Decided to give it another two hours and call it a day. Two hours later, it was six hours since I had started my experiment. I looked at the water in the glass and yes! there was a hint, only a slight hint, but a definite tinge of pink in it.

I tasted it. It wasn't rosé; it was hot water, tasting of hot water. But the interesting part was that it was very hot indeed, and had begun slowly bubbling.

Since I had spent so many hours putting healing energies into it, I decided to drink it anyway. I didn't have lift-off, but I'm positive it gave me more energy!

Expanding Tight Rings

I have often used energy to expand tight-fitting gold rings so that the wearers could remove them. The process is simple. I ask the person to place his or her hand on a table, and after a few minutes of mentally projecting energy towards the ring it can easily be removed.

About the fifth time I did this I was having a drink with an associate of Alan's when he mentioned that he couldn't get his signet ring off his little finger. I suggested that he place his hand flat on the table between us so that I could project energy towards it.

Five minutes later, he was able to remove the ring with ease. Alan eventually drove him back to work, and during this time he remarked once or twice that the ring was still expanding! What he hadn't told me was that he had also been unable to remove his wedding ring – ever since his marriage, in fact. This ring also expanded, and he was able to take it off as well.

To this day his signet ring is so loose that it almost falls off, and he can still remove his wedding ring.

The Poinsettia Plant

I was given a poinsettia plant one Christmas, and when the flowers had finally died I thought I would see how long I could make it last without water, by feeding it energy alone. I decided to project energy to it every day.

I gave instructions to my family to keep away from it, and not to feel sorry for it! Everyone observed the rules. I didn't make a specific time for treating the plant, but zipped some energy to it two or three times a day as I walked past it. After six months the compost it was in was as hard as concrete, yet the plant's leaves were soft and pliant, and there were six new soft green leaves.

After seven months I began to feel sorry for it myself, so I planted it in a sheltered corner of the garden and gradually began giving it water. It was still flourishing three years later.

Dispersing Clouds

One day Michael Bentine said to me: 'With all your power, you could disperse clouds!' Michael himself has often demonstrated this feat in his garden. He can also make it rain, which I haven't yet achieved. But when he suggested that I might be able to disperse clouds I went away and tried it. To my amazement, it worked!

The secret seems to lie in first finding the right mental wavelength; I then use my 'laser beam' technique, directing it into the cloud until it completely disappears.

When Alan and I spent a weekend away in Dorset, we stood on a cliff-top looking up at the sky one day, trying to determine whether it would stay fine. It was slightly cloudy, so I said: 'I'll get rid of a few of those clouds if you like!' Alan laughed, obviously thinking I was quite mad.

I gave him a demonstration, and the clouds vanished. Alan remarked sceptically that the air-currents would have taken them away anyway. So I spent the day inviting him to pick which cloud I should work on; he chose harder and harder ones, many of them in the middle of other cloud-masses. By the end of the day, when I had dispersed every cloud he chose, he was finally convinced!

Then there was the time when we were returning to Athens by coach after spending a wonderful day at Delphi – which is a very psychic place indeed. Our coach was held up in a traffic jam, so to pass the time Alan suggested that I should work on the clouds. As usual, he set me a very difficult task. He chose a cluster of four large clouds surrounded by a cloud-mass: I was to remove the four inner clouds.

I had been working on them for about eight minutes when the coach started to move. By this time three and a half clouds had been dispersed, so I quickly pointed my finger at the remaining half-cloud, and it instantly went! The cloud-mass around was still intact and hadn't moved.

If you want to try this yourself, start with small fluffy clouds. It is best to watch them carefully for about fifteen minutes to make absolutely certain they are not dispersing of their own accord. If they are still there at the end of this time, then you can begin.

Imagine a 'laser beam' of energy from your mind going straight into the cloud. Then move it about, and *know* without any shadow of doubt that it will disappear.

Keep your energy games positive, remembering Universal Law; if you use energy with any kind of destructive intent it will come back to you.

At one time, during the Uri Geller era, I tried to bend spoons and forks; however, I had an inner doubt as to whether I could do it, and also as to whether I *should* use energy to distort things – and I failed miserably. I also doubted whether I would be able to succeed with the water-into-wine experiment; although I spent a long time on it, I really didn't think it would happen.

It is an interesting fact that if I have known without any shadow of doubt that an experiment would be successful it always was. If I have had any doubt in my mind whatsoever, or feared that it might fail, then it has failed. There is obviously a very definite link between positivity and success, and between negativity and failure, which is always demonstrated in any kind of test that harnesses energies.

There is a very powerful message here!

A FINAL WORD

For thirteen years I have worked as a medium, healer, hypnotherapist and vitamin and mineral therapist. From the beginning I set out to find the truth about the whole spectrum of healing skills and mediumship that I have described in this book.

As well as experiencing these for myself, I have studied the claims made by other mediums and healers over the past century about survival evidence, clairvoyance, healing and absent healing. They are, in my opinion, absolutely truthful.

In my investigation into truth I have been given a bonus in the form of my clairvoyant sight of mind energy. This discovery, by leading me into further investigations into the potential of the mind, has radically changed the direction of my work.

I now teach and lecture on the mind and its potential, and give demonstrations of healing the energy counterpart. Most important of all, I am still discovering what my own potential may be, for no matter how far along the road I have come I know that I am still only at the beginning, and I shall continue my investigations.

It is up to every one of us to seek knowledge, improve the power of our mind, and discover what we are really capable of. With the expansion of the mind come health, excitement and positivity and, very important, independence and self-reliance. I hope this book will inspire you to have a go. Most important of all, never give up. Keep trying. Life is full of fascinating things waiting for *you* to discover them.

If you would like to contact Betty Shine, please write to:

> PO Box 1009
> Hassocks
> West Sussex
> BN6 8XS

You may also be interested to know that Betty Shine has recorded several tapes about her work and self-help. For more information, please send an S.A.E. to the above address.

Also available from Corgi Books:

MIND MAGIC

BY BETTY SHINE

A natural extension of her talks, lectures and private consultations, Betty Shine's second book is a self-help guide that will enable everyone to experience the benefits of mind energy and healing.

0 552 13671 9

Bibliography

Benham, William G., *Laws of Scientific Hand Reading*, Tarporevala, Bombay, 1975.

Bhaktivendanta, Swami Prabhupada, *Bhagavad Gita*, Bhaktivendanta Book Trust, London and Sydney, 1968.

Davies, Dr Stephen and Stewart, Dr Alan, *Nutritional Medicine*, Pan Books, London and Sydney, 1987.

Deshpande, P. Y., *The Authentic Yoga*, Rider & Company, London, 1982.

Garde, Dr R. K., *Yoga Therapy*, Wolfe, New Delhi, 1973.

Harris, Bertha, *Traveller in Eternity*, Regency Press, London and New York, 1956, reprinted in 1975.

Harrison, Peter and Mary, *Life Before Birth*, Futura Macdonald & Co., London and Sydney, 1983.

Hittleman, Richard, *Guide to Yoga Meditation*, Bantam Books, London, New York, Toronto, 1969.

Hoyle, Fred and Wickramasinghe, N. C., *Diseases From Space*, Sphere Books, London, 1979.

Iyengar, B. K. S., *Light on Yoga*, Allen & Unwin, London, 1968.

Jaquin, Noel, *The Hand Speaks*, Sagar Publications, New Delhi, 1973.

Meek, George W. and Harris, Bertha, *Seance To Science*, Regency Press, London and New York, 1973.

Ouseley, S. G. J., *The Power of the Rays: The Science of Colour Healing*, L. N. Fowler & Co. Ltd., London, 1975.

Reiker, Hans-Ulrich, *The Yoga Of Light*, The Dawn Horse Press, California, 1976.

Schul, Bill, *The Psychic Power of Animals*, Coronet Books, London, 1977.

Wolff, Charlotte, *The Hand In Psychological Diagnosis*, Sagar Publications, New Delhi, 1972.

FINDING A MEDIUM

Appointments can be made with mediums and the following organizations:

The College of Psychic Studies, 16 Queensberry Place, London SW7 2EB. Tel. 071-589-3292.

The Spiritualist Association of Great Britain, 33 Belgrave Square, London SW1X 8QB. Tel. 071-235-3351.